DISCLAI

01

Table Of Contents

Introduction ———————————————— 03

Chapter 1

HISTORY AND ORIGIN OF CROCHET ——————— 06

Chapter 2

ALL THE TOOLS, MATERIALS AND TECHNIQUES

FROM CHOOSING A HOOK AND YARN TO

SEAMING ———————————————— 18

Chapter 3

Basic Crochet Stitches ——————————— 28

Chapter 4

Crochet Kitchen Items ——————————— 44

Chapter 5

Crochet Personal Items ——————————— 51

Chapter 6

Crochet Home Decor Items —————————— 61

Chapter 7

Crochet for Kids ————————————— 75

Chapter 8

Important things for beginners ———————— 99

Chapter 9

Tips For Every Novice Crocheter ———————— 104

Introduction

Crochet, derived from the French word "crochet" meaning a hook, is an art form that has been passed down through generations. This timeless craft not only provides entertainment but also brings a sense of calmness to those who practice it. The best part? It's incredibly easy to learn! With just a crochet hook and some thread or yarn, you can create stunning clothing and home decoration items, ranging from hats, tops, scarves, and ponchos to tablecloths, bedspreads, and doilies. And let's not forget the adorable pieces designed specifically for kids, making crochet a trendy needle craft for all ages.

To get started with crochet, you only need two basic supplies: a crochet hook and your choice of thread or yarn. Most crochet stitches involve wrapping the thread or yarn around the hook in a sequence of yarn overs or thread wraps. Once you've mastered the single crochet stitch, the others will come effortlessly! While most designs begin with a slip stitch and a sequence of loops called chains, you can even learn to build foundations without following the conventional chain method. Crochet designs are created in rows, where you crochet back and forth, building each row on top of the previous one, or in circles, where you work around a middle ring of loops, forming geometric shapes like circles, hexagons, or rectangles. Each motif is a piece of geometry that you make as many times as needed, and then you sew them all together to shape your final product.

Crochet has a rich history that dates back centuries. In the sixteenth century, nuns taught crochet to their graduates, considering it a valuable skill and a symbol of high birth. During that time, crochet was primarily associated with wealthy individuals, while knitting was more commonly used by those less fortunate. However, in the early 1800s, crochet started gaining popularity as fabrics made from lace became more expensive than crochet products. It's interesting to note that the art of crochet developed independently in two distinct milieus in Europe.

Before the 1840s, crochet patterns were handed down within families, with each generation passing on the skill to the next. Wooden hooks made from bones or old spoons were used to create the early 19th-century version of crochet, known as shepherd's knitting. Around the same time, another style of crochet emerged from a needlework technique called tambourine, which involved a small hooked needle used on fabric stretched over a work-frame. The transition from tambourine to crochet involved abandoning the fabric and executing the looped chain stitch "in the air."

Crochet has not only served as an artistic expression but has also been used by different societies to signify social class. The ability to afford crochet products and lace-crafted items was seen as a status symbol. Interestingly, crochet requires less expensive materials and equipment, such as threads and yarns readily available at local stores.

There have been debates about the origin of crochet, with some experts suggesting countries like Saudi Arabia, Brazil, and China based on the cultural background of their traditional clothing. Additionally, it's been proposed that the technique of crocheting was more about the dexterity of the forefinger rather than the creation of crochet and knitted products.

During the nineteenth century, crochet continued to evolve in Europe and the United States, mainly as a female activity. Women's magazines of that time featured a variety of crochet designs, ranging from traditional clothing items like blouses, bonnets, collars, scarves, and babywear to intricate creations like birdcage coverings. Museums house a wealth of crocheted bags and purses from the latter half of the 19th century, with some of the finest examples being the miser bags made with colored sil

Chapter 1

HISTORY AND ORIGIN OF CROCHET

The history of crochet is shrouded in mystery, with limited information available about its earliest origins. It is believed that the earliest form of crochet may have been created using fingers rather than the hooks we use today. Some theories suggest that crochet could have existed as early as 1500 BC, as part of religious devotees' work, which included needlepoint lace and bobbin lace.

There are three main theories regarding the origin of crochet. One theory suggests that it originated in Arabia and spread eastward to Tibet and then westward to Spain, eventually following the Arab trade routes to other Mediterranean countries. Another theory proposes that it originated in South America, where an indigenous tribe used crochet ornaments in coming-of-age ceremonies. A third alternative stems from the fact that early examples of crochet dolls were known in China.

However, there is no solid evidence to determine the true age or origin of crochet. The evidence of its existence in the 16th century is scarce and highly debated. References to a type of "anchored cutting" appear around 1580, but this seems to have been a form of stitching onto fabric resembling intricate braiding.

During the Renaissance, women would crochet several strands of thread together, creating fabrics similar to lace. The earliest evidence of crochet, as we know it today, is commonly found in the second half of the 18th century. Crochet may have evolved from Chinese embroidery, an ancient form of weaving known in Turkey, India, Persia, and North Africa, which reached Europe in the 18th century and was referred to as tambouring.

The main hypothesis regarding the origin of crochet suggests that it began when it was realized that chains worked in a pattern could interlock without a fabric background. By the end of the 18th century, tambour evolved into what the French called "crochet in the air," where the fabric background was eliminated, and the stitches were worked on their own. Tambour hooks were as small as sewing needles, indicating that the work was likely done with fine thread.

Crochet has a fascinating history that has evolved over time. In the mid-nineteenth century, crochet began to develop in Europe, thanks to the efforts of Mlle Riego de la Branchardiere. She transformed needlepoint lace and bobbin lace designs into crochet patterns that could be replicated. Mlle Riego de la Branchardiere published numerous patterns and claimed to have invented a lace-like crochet known today as Irish crochet.

Some researchers believe that crochet originated in China as a form of embroidery called "tambouring." While it was not used to create afghan blankets and throws like crochet is used today, its interlocking weaving of yarn may have paved the way for modern crochet. Instead of using a hook, tambouring employed a thin needle that created a stitched lace. This could have been the precursor to the delicate fabrics used to make baby afghans to keep children warm.

Another theory suggests that crochet originated in the sixteenth century in England and France. During this time, crochet was not used to create the crocheted afghans and throws we know today. Instead, it was used to make chains of delicate lace. Fine homemade thread was used to create intricate patterns that were highly valued.

Although these early forms of crochet predate the crochet hook, the first substantial evidence of modern crochet was not found until the nineteenth century. At that time, making a crochet afghan or throw was done entirely by hand, using fingers to manipulate the thread. It took many hours and skilled fingers to create a crocheted afghan without the use of a hook.

As the art of crochet evolved and the use of hooks became more prevalent, making beautiful afghans and custom covers became easier. Crochet hooks, made of materials such as steel, plastic, or aluminum, replaced the earlier ivory, wood, or bone hooks. These modern crochet hooks come in a variety of sizes to achieve different patterns often found in crochet afghans. With the aid of these hooks, creating a custom afghan or throw became faster, easier, and more precise.

Crochet gained popularity as an alternative to knitting, allowing people to create custom afghan blankets for their beds or soft baby afghans to give as gifts. The availability of literature, such as magazines and books with crochet patterns, further enabled individuals to learn and create their own crocheted afghans without the need for an instructor.

However, during World War II, resources and materials became scarce, and the demand for crochet decreased. Many women who previously made crochet baby afghans and tended to their households were now employed in factories, leaving little time for afghan-making. After the war, although the nation recovered, the demand for custom afghan covers remained low.

In the 1970s, crochet experienced a resurgence in popularity. The relaxed fashion styles of the time made crocheted vests, sweaters, and accessories highly sought after. Both men and women were learning to crochet and creating a wide range of items, from baby afghans to belts and scarves. The availability of vibrant yarn colors and the abundance of crochet instruction in magazines contributed to the renewed interest in crochet as a means of self-expression.

During this time, the therapeutic benefits of crochet also became apparent. As interest in psychology grew, it was discovered that crocheting afghans, like many hobbies, helped reduce stress. Creating a crochet baby afghan or working on an afghan blanket could provide a sense of relaxation and produce a beautiful end product.

Crocheting afghans is relatively easy to learn, with increasingly complex styles and patterns that can be mastered with practice. It can be self-taught or learned through classes offered at craft stores. Books and magazines provide endless ideas for new afghan patterns and delicate crochet baby afghans

Crocheting is a skill that involves holding a crochet hook in one hand and manipulating the yarn with the other hand. This creates interlocking loops of yarn, forming a chain. The chain is then worked back and forth, using yarn from the previous chain to create subsequent chains and build the desired structure, whether it's a baby afghan, clothing, or even stuffed animals like teddy bears. There are various stitches used in crocheting afghans, but the most common ones are single crochet, double crochet, and triple crochet. The intricate patterns achieved in crochet afghans and throws come from varying the types of stitches used while working. The more stitch variety in crochet afghans, the more detailed and interesting the pattern becomes.

One of the easiest items to crochet is an afghan or a scarf. Beginners can start by using a single color of yarn and practicing their craft. Once comfortable with crocheting, a beginner can easily create a crochet baby afghan or afghan throw in just a few hours.

The beauty of crochet is that it can be done anywhere with just a few simple tools: yarn and a crochet hook. With the ease of learning and the popularity of crochet afghans and baby afghans as homemade gifts, this craft is likely to be passed down through generations. For every crochet baby afghan that is made, the art will be taught to someone new, ensuring its continuation and allowing others to learn and appreciate it.

Crochet and the Irish Connection

During the devastating Great Irish Famine that occurred from 1845 to 1849, Ursuline Nuns in Ireland began teaching local women and children the art of thread crochet. The items they made were then exported and sold in America and Europe. This marked the emergence of a style of crochet now commonly known as Irish lace, which played a crucial role in helping many Irish families survive the famine. A cottage industry developed around crochet, particularly in Ireland and Northern

France. As these items were purchased by the emerging middle class in Europe, the upper class began to view crochet as a cheap imitation of lace suitable for the general public. They promoted the older style of lace made through more expensive methods as being superior.

The popularity of Irish lace crochet continued to grow, and it became an important source of income for many families. Skilled lace makers created intricate and delicate designs using fine threads. Irish crochet lace, characterized by its three-dimensional motifs and decorative elements, gained recognition and admiration internationally. The exquisite craftsmanship of Irish lace became synonymous with luxury and elegance.

Crochet Becomes an Art Form

The emergence of crochet as an art form in its own right gained momentum in the twentieth century. Queen Victoria's adoption of crochet helped remove some of the stigma associated with the craft. As patterns became more widely available, a standardized stitch size became essential. Crochet hooks began to be manufactured in various sizes to accommodate the specific thread or yarn thickness required by the pattern.

The 12 Cluster Initiative on Crochet refers to a collective effort to promote and advance the art of crochet. This initiative aims to bring together crochet enthusiasts, designers, and artisans to share knowledge, exchange ideas, and collaborate on projects. By fostering a sense of community and encouraging creativity, the 12 Cluster Initiative seeks to elevate crochet to new heights and preserve its rich tradition.A

Through the initiative, crocheters can explore new techniques, experiment with different patterns, and showcase their creations. Workshops, exhibitions, and online platforms provide opportunities for individuals to connect, learn, and celebrate the art of crochet. The 12 Cluster Initiative on Crochet plays a vital role in supporting and nurturing the growth of this timeless craft in the modern era.

Crochet Continues to Evolve

The history of crochet continues to evolve as a new generation of crocheters brings forth new stitches, techniques, and designs. The availability of magazines and books dedicated to crochet has further enhanced its popularity and accessibility. These publications provide a wealth of patterns, tutorials, and inspiration for crocheters of all levels.

Moreover, the world of yarn has expanded exponentially, with an incredible variety of yarns now available in various styles, weights, and colors. From natural fibers like wool and cotton to synthetic blends and novelty yarns, crocheters have an endless array of choices to suit their projects and personal preferences.

In addition to the creative possibilities offered by yarn and patterns, the crochet hook itself has become a work of art. Craftsmen now produce crochet hooks in a multitude of styles, sizes, and materials. From beautifully carved wooden hooks to smooth acrylic ones, and even hooks made from polymer clay, there is a hook to suit every crocheter's individual taste and ergonomic needs.

This ongoing evolution in crochet reflects the passion and creativity of the global crochet community. With the availability of resources, materials, and tools, crocheters are able to push the boundaries of the craft, experiment with new techniques, and create stunning works of art. The future of crochet holds endless possibilities as it continues to inspire and captivate crocheters around the world.

Yarn

Yarn is the essential material used in crochet and is available in various forms. It is commonly sold as balls or skeins (hanks), although it may also be wound on spools or cones. Skeins and balls of yarn are typically accompanied by a yarn band, which provides important information about the yarn, such as its weight, length, color lot, fiber content, washing instructions, recommended needle size, gauge, and more. Crocheters often keep the yarn band for future reference, especially when additional skeins are needed. It is important to ensure that the yarn for a project comes from the same color lot to maintain consistent color throughout the work. If additional yarn of the same color lot is required, it can usually be obtained from other yarn stores or online.

The thickness or weight of the yarn, often referred to as the gauge, is a crucial factor in determining the number of stitches and rows needed to cover a given area in a specific stitch pattern. Thicker yarns typically require larger crochet hooks, while thinner yarns can be crocheted with thicker or thinner hooks. As a result, thicker yarns generally require fewer stitches and less time to complete a project. The recommended gauge for a particular yarn can be found on the label that wraps around the skein when purchased in stores. Patterns and motifs may appear bolder and more pronounced with thicker yarns, while thinner yarns are better suited for delicate or intricate pattern work. Yarns are commonly categorized into six thickness categories: superfine, fine, light, medium, bulky, and super bulky. Quantitatively, thickness is measured by the number of wraps per inch (WPI), and the weight per unit length is typically measured in tex or denier.

Before use, hanks of yarn are often wound into balls to make crocheting easier and prevent the yarn from becoming tangled. This winding process can be done by hand or with the help of a ballwinder and swift, which allows the yarn to be neatly wound into a center-pull ball.

The usefulness of a yarn is determined by several factors, including its loft (ability to trap air), elasticity (resistance to stretching), launderability, colorfastness, hand (feel and texture, such as softness or scratchiness), durability against abrasion, resistance to pilling, fuzziness, tendency to twist or untwist, overall weight and drape, blocking and felting properties, comfort (breathability, moisture absorption, and wicking properties), and appearance, which encompasses color, sheen, smoothness, and any decorative features. Other factors to consider include allergenicity, drying speed, resistance to chemicals, moths, and mildew, melting point and flammability, static cling, and the ability to accept dyes. Desired properties may vary depending on the project, so there is no one "best" yarn for all purposes.

While crochet can be done with materials such as fabric strips, metal wire, or more exotic fibers, most yarns used in crochet are made through spinning. Spinning involves twisting fibers to create yarn that resists breaking under tension. The twisting can be done in either direction, resulting in a Z-twist or S-twist yarn. If the fibers are aligned by brushing and the spinner uses a worsted drafting technique, such as the short forward draw, the resulting yarn is smoother and known as worsted-spun. On the other hand, if the fibers are carded but not brushed and the spinner uses a woolen drafting technique, such as the long backward draw, the resulting yarn is fuzzier and known as woolen-spun.

Yarn can be composed of continuous fiber strands, such as silk and many synthetic fibers, or it can be made of staple fibers, which are fibers of a fixed length, usually a few inches. Fiber strands are sometimes cut into staples before spinning. The strength of spun yarn against breaking is determined by the amount of twist, the length of the fibers, and the thickness of the yarn. Generally, yarns become stronger with more twist, longer fibers, and thicker yarns (more strands). Thinner yarns require more twist than thicker yarns to resist breaking under tension. The thickness of the yarn may vary along its length, and a slub refers to a thicker section where a mass of fibers is joined into the yarn.

The fibers used in yarn can be classified into animal fibers, plant fibers, and synthetic fibers. Animal fibers include silk as well as the long hairs of animals such as sheep (wool), goats (angora or cashmere), rabbits (angora), llamas, alpacas, dogs, cats, camels, yaks, and muskoxen (qiviut). Plants used for fibers include cotton, flax (for linen), bamboo, ramie, hemp, jute, nettle, raffia, yucca, coconut husk, banana trees, soy, and corn. Rayon and acetate fibers are also produced from cellulose, primarily derived from trees. Common synthetic fibers include acrylics, polyesters like dacron and ingeo, nylon and other polyamides, and olefins such as polypropylene. Among these types, wool is often preferred for crochet due to its superior elasticity, warmth, and, at times, felting properties. However, wool can be less convenient to clean and some individuals may be allergic to it. It is also common to blend different fibers in a yarn, such as 85% alpaca and 15% silk. Even within a particular type of fiber, there can be great variety in the length and thickness of the fibers. For example, Merino wool and Egyptian cotton are favored because they produce exceptionally long, thin (fine) fibers for their respective types.

A single spun yarn can be used as it is or plied with another yarn. Plying involves spinning two or more yarns together, usually in the opposite direction from which they were spun individually. For example, two Z-twist yarns are commonly plied with an S-twist. The plying twist reduces the tendency of the yarns to twist and produces a thicker, balanced yarn. Used yarns may themselves be plied together, resulting in cabled yarns or multi-stranded yarns. Occasionally, the yarns being used are fed at different rates, causing one yarn to loop around the other, as in bouclé. The single yarns may be dyed separately before use or dyed afterward to give the yarn a uniform appearance.

The dyeing of yarn is a complex art. Yarns can be left undyed or dyed a single color, or they can be dyed in a wide range of colors. Dyeing can be done mechanically, by hand, or even hand-painted onto the yarn. A wide variety of synthetic dyes have been developed since the invention of indigo dye in the mid-nineteenth century. However, natural dyes are also possible, although they generally produce less vibrant colors. The color scheme of a yarn is sometimes referred to as its colorway. Variegated yarns, which have multiple colors in a repeating pattern, can create interesting visual effects such as diagonal stripes.

Chapter 2

ALL THE TOOLS, MATERIALS AND TECHNIQUES FROM CHOOSING A HOOK AND YARN TO SEAMING

When I first started crocheting 20 years ago, I only had a few skeins of yarn and two crochet hooks. These two main materials are all you really need to begin crocheting. However, as your crocheting becomes a hobby, passion, or even a business, you will find the need for more essential tools and better preparation.

Crocheting is one of the most affordable hobbies to start with. But be warned, once you start, you might become addicted to all the beautiful yarn and find yourself with a growing stash! For now, let's focus on the basic crochet materials and supplies you need to get started. Along with yarn and a crochet hook, I'll also mention a few others that can make your crocheting experience a bit easier.

The essential materials and supplies you need to start with crochet are:

Yarn: Choose a yarn that suits your project. There are countless varieties available, ranging from different fiber types, weights, and colors. Start with a medium-weight yarn, such as worsted weight, as it is versatile and easy to work with.

Crochet Hook(s): Select crochet hooks in various sizes to accommodate different yarn weights and achieve the desired tension. The hook size you need will depend on the thickness of the yarn you are using. Common hook sizes range from 2.25mm to 6.5mm. You can start with a basic set of hooks or buy individual hooks as needed.

Tapestry Needle: Also known as a darning needle or yarn needle, this large-eyed needle is used for weaving in yarn ends and joining crochet pieces together. It's essential for finishing your projects neatly.

Stitch Markers (optional): Stitch markers can be helpful in marking specific stitches or sections in your work, especially in complex patterns. They can be small rings or clips that you place on your crochet stitches to keep track of your progress.

Hook Case (optional, but highly recommended): As your collection of crochet hooks grows, it's beneficial to have a hook case or organizer to keep them organized and easily accessible. It helps prevent hooks from getting lost or damaged and makes it convenient to bring your hooks along with you.

With these basic crochet materials and supplies, you have everything you need to get started on your crochet journey. As you progress and explore more complex projects, you may find the need for additional tools such as stitch counters, measuring tapes, or blocking mats. But for now, enjoy the simplicity and creativity that crochet brings with just these essentials.

You're absolutely right! Yarn is an essential component of crochet, and there are so many options to choose from. The type of yarn you select can greatly impact the final texture and appearance of your project, whether it's a garment, home decor item, or toy.

Yarn is categorized based on its weight and the fibers used. There are various types of yarn fibers available, including polyester, acrylic, wool, cotton, superwash merino, and many more. Each type of fiber has its own unique characteristics and qualities.

Yarn weight refers to the thickness and heaviness of the yarn. There are seven weight categories: Lace (0), Superfine (1), Fine (2), DK/Light (3), Medium (4, also known as worsted weight), Bulky (5), Super Bulky (6), and Jumbo (7). The weight of the yarn affects the drape, stitch definition, and the overall look of your crochet project.

When you're just starting out, I recommend using a medium weight yarn (worsted weight) as it is versatile, widely available, and easy to work with. It's also a good choice because it allows you to see your stitches clearly and provides a good balance between speed and detail.

Some of my favorite medium weight yarns include Lion Brand Vanna's Choice and Wool-Ease. They offer a wide range of colors and are known for their durability and softness. Another popular choice is Red Heart Super Saver, which is great for fun and vibrant projects like the Trick or Treat Witch Backpack you mentioned.

As you become more experienced in crochet, you can explore other yarn weights and fibers to add more variety and texture to your creations. Remember to have fun and experiment with different yarns to find the ones that you enjoy working with and that suit your project's needs. Happy crocheting!

Crochet Hooks

Absolutely! It's common for people to get confused between knitting and crochet, but let me clarify the differences for you. The main distinction between knitting and crochet lies in the tools used. Knitting involves using two pointed needles, whereas crochet is done with a single hooked needle.

In crochet, there are various types of hooks available, each with its own characteristics. Some common types of crochet hooks include aluminum, bamboo, ergonomic, plastic, and handmade ones. The choice of hook material is often a personal preference, and you may find that you prefer different hooks for different projects.

When it comes to crochet hooks, I have a collection of various sizes, types, and brands. Starting with a beginner's set is a great way to get started, and as you gain experience, you can experiment with different hooks to see which ones you prefer for different projects.

When purchasing a hook for a specific yarn, it's important to ensure that the size of the hook matches the recommended size on the yarn label. The recommended hook size is usually indicated on the yarn label to help you achieve the desired tension and gauge for your project.

By using the correct hook size for your yarn, you can ensure that your stitches are the right size and your finished project turns out as intended. Over time, you'll develop a sense of which hooks work best for you and your preferred crochet techniques.

So remember, knitting uses two pointed needles, while crochet is done with a single hooked needle. Choose your crochet hook based on your preference and the recommended hook size for your yarn. Happy crocheting!

Ergonomic Hooks

Ergonomic hooks can be a game-changer for those who experience wrist or hand fatigue or cramping while crocheting. These hooks are designed with a grip or handle that reduces the strain on your hand, allowing for more comfortable and extended crocheting sessions.

While you may not have felt the need for ergonomic hooks in the past, trying out different brands and styles can bring about new discoveries. Clover Crochet Hooks, for example, are highly regarded for their ergonomic design and may provide a better experience for those with hand or wrist issues.

If you're interested in exploring more crochet tools and resources, I recommend joining the email list mentioned. By signing up, you'll receive a variety of freebies and goodies, including a list of the author's favorite crochet tools and resources. It's a great way to stay updated and discover new helpful items for your crochet journey.

So, if you've been experiencing any discomfort or want to enhance your crocheting experience, consider giving ergonomic hooks a try. And don't forget to join the email list to access valuable resources and receive even more crochet-related goodies. Happy crocheting!

Aluminum and Plastic

Aluminum and plastic hooks are affordable options that come in a wide range of sizes, making them versatile choices for crocheters. Both types of hooks have their advantages.

Aluminum hooks are known for their durability and strength. They glide smoothly through the yarn, making it easy to work your stitches. They are particularly well-suited for projects that require a bit more tension or working with thicker yarns. Aluminum hooks are a popular choice among crocheters and are readily available in various sizes.

Plastic hooks, on the other hand, are lightweight and often more budget-friendly than other types of hooks. They can work well for many projects, especially with lighter weight yarns. However, as you mentioned, plastic hooks may have limitations when it comes to certain situations. When crocheting with two strands of yarn or with cotton yarn, the extra tension and resistance may put more stress on the plastic hook, making it more prone to bending or even breaking.

It's important to consider the specific requirements of your project and the type of yarn you're using when selecting a hook. For projects that require more strength or involve heavier yarns, aluminum hooks may be a better choice. However, if you're working with lighter yarns and don't require as much tension, plastic hooks can still work well.

Ultimately, it's a matter of personal preference and finding what works best for you and your crochet style. Trying out different types of hooks and materials can help you determine which ones suit your needs and provide the most enjoyable crocheting experience.

Carefully assembled Hooks

It's important to do thorough research and read reviews before purchasing a handmade hook. This will help ensure that you're investing in a high-quality product that meets your specific needs. Reviews can provide valuable insights into the craftsmanship, durability, and performance of the hook, giving you a better idea of what to expect.

Additionally, handmade hooks offer a wide variety of designs and styles, allowing you to find a hook that truly reflects your personality and preferences. Whether you're drawn to a colorful clay handle or the natural beauty of a wooden one, the options are endless.

Embroidered artwork Needle

A tapestry needle, also known as a darning needle or yarn needle, is an essential tool in crochet. It resembles a sewing needle but has a larger eye and a blunt tip, making it safe to use with yarn.

After completing your crochet project and tying off the yarn, the tapestry needle is used to weave in the loose ends or seams. This process helps secure the yarn and gives your project a polished and finished look. By threading the yarn through the eye of the needle, you can seamlessly hide the loose ends within the stitches of your work.

Tapestry needles come in various sizes, so it's a good idea to have a few different ones on hand to accommodate different yarn weights and thicknesses. Choosing the right size needle ensures that the yarn can easily pass through the stitches without causing any distortion.

With the help of a tapestry needle, you can neatly and securely finish off your crochet projects, making them ready for use or gifting. It's a simple yet essential tool that every crocheter should have in their kit.

Snare Case

Having a case or storage solution for your crochet supplies is definitely a helpful addition to your crochet toolkit. It provides a convenient and organized way to keep all your hooks, yarn, and accessories in one place.

There are various options available for crochet cases, ranging from compact pouches to larger tote bags or even specialized crochet hook organizers. You can find them at local craft stores, online marketplaces like Amazon, or even handmade cases on platforms like Etsy.

When selecting a case, consider the size and compartments that will best suit your needs. Look for features like pockets, slots, or zippered compartments to keep your hooks, yarn needles, stitch markers, and other small accessories secure and easily accessible. Some cases may also have designated spaces for holding yarn, preventing it from tangling or unraveling.

Having a dedicated case for your crochet supplies not only keeps everything organized but also makes it convenient to take your projects on the go. Whether you're attending a crochet group or simply want to crochet while traveling, a case ensures that you have everything you need in one portable package.

So, if you find yourself accumulating more crochet supplies and want to keep them in order, consider investing in a case or storage solution that suits your preferences and helps you maintain a tidy and efficient crochet space.

Join Markers

YStitch markers are small, often removable, markers that help you keep track of specific points or stitches in your crochet work.

Here are a few instances where stitch markers can come in handy:

Tracking Rows: In larger projects where you need to keep count of your rows, stitch markers can be placed at specific intervals to mark the end of each row. This can be especially helpful when working on blankets, scarves, or garments, ensuring that you don't lose track of your progress.

Crocheting in the Round: When working in continuous rounds, such as in amigurumi or hats, a stitch marker can be used to mark the first stitch of each round. This helps you keep your place and ensures that you maintain the correct stitch count in each round.

Shaping and Construction: Stitch markers can be used to mark important points when shaping a garment, such as armholes or necklines. They can also be used to hold pieces together while sewing or joining panels, making the assembly process easier and more precise.

Stitch markers can be as simple as safety pins, small pieces of contrasting yarn, or specialized markers designed specifically for crochet. They can be easily moved or removed as needed, allowing you to adjust their placement as your project progresses.

While stitch markers may not be essential for every project, having a set on hand can be beneficial in many situations, saving you time and helping you maintain accuracy in your crochet work. As you gain more experience and take on more complex projects, you'll likely find stitch markers to be an invaluable tool in your crochet toolkit.

Chapter 3

BASIC CROCHET STITCHES

Slip knot:

To create the very first loop on your hook (named as a slipknot), start by crossing the yarn that falls from the ball over the yarns other ends (termed as the yarn's tail) to create a yarn ring.

PUSH THE HOOK SIDE into the circle of yarn. Now using the hook, catch the yarn's ball end and draw the yarn into the circular loop.

THIS CREATES A LOOP on your hook and a loose, free knot underneath your loop.

PULL BOTH THE ENDS of your thread tightly to secure the knot and loop across the shank of your hook.

ENSURE THAT THE FINISHED slipknot is secure enough to the hook to prevent it from slipping off, but not so rigid that you may barely slide it down the shank of your hook. The yarn tail on your slipknot will be at least be 6in (15 cm) in length so that it may be connected to the blunt-ended yarn needle and then darned later on. This creates your first slip knot.

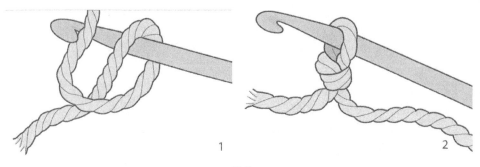

1   2

CHAIN STITCHES:

Chain stitches are the first crochet stitch that you have to know, as they stitches form the basis for all your other stitches—this stitch is also called a base chain—and for turning strings. Combined with other simple stitches they are used to construct a large variety of crochet stitch designs, including thick layered stitches and lacy ones.

Making a foundation chain:

Begin at the hook with a slip knot. Tie the yarn around your hook; in crochet techniques, this movement is called "yarn over your hook." If you're making a Y.O.H move, push your hook under the yarn while pulling the yarn gently forward.

PULL A LOOP OF YARN on the hook with the yarn clenched in the edge of the hook. (Hold the slipknot center with your thread hands-free fingers while you pull the loop through it).
THIS FINISHES OFF THE first chain.
NOW DRAW A LOOP FOR each new stitch around the loop hook. Continue to create chains the very same manner till your crochet design has the number of chains specified in your pattern.

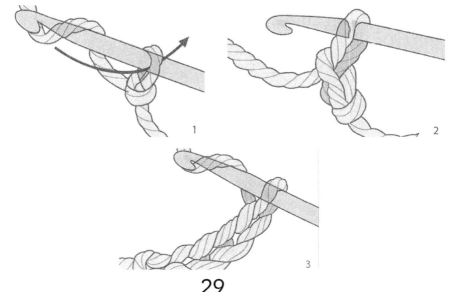

ADDING SINGLE CROCHET in your Foundation Chain

1.Thread the hook beneath the first strand of the 2nd chain on the hook. Yarn over it and draw a circle, yarn over it again, and bring your hook into the leftover 2 loops.

2.Precede this way, putting the hook underneath another chain's top strand and making a single crochet stitch afterward. Working your way, though, before ten full crochets have been done.

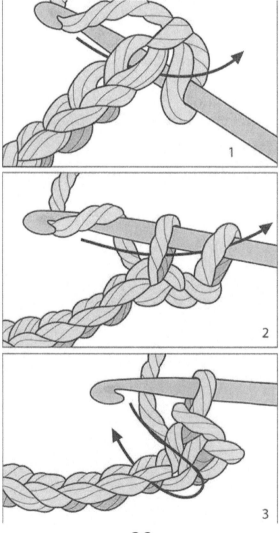

COUNTING THE STITCH:

Analyzing the 1st row by taking a second to look at the base chain stitches you've just created. We will notice that every stitch has 2 legs going down; also, the "toes" are both pointing together until they vanish through the base chain and create a V like a shape.

There you will even notice that every stitch on the top edge of it has a line that looks like another chain; this will be the front ("right") side of your stitch itself. Then, flip over 1 turning chain and flip the entire work over. Look to the other side of every stitch once more. See that both the legs point away from one another, and in the end, there is an additional line horizontally across the 2 legs below the cord. This is your stitch's backside. It resembles a little like the sign of pi (π).

MAKE A FEW MORE ROWS, turn and keep on working, and afterward take a good look at the article you were creating. Remember that the front and back sides of your stitches are colored differently. In your work, you may notice alternating rows of such kinds. It is possible to misinterpret these 2 rows as just a single row of stitch at a glance, like piled Lincoln Logs. However, if you have a closer look at the stitch, you can identify the design on the front and backside of the design.

HALF DOUBLE CROCHET STITCHES:

Before you start practicing all of the extra stitches in this section, it's essential to realize that you have already completed much of the tough work! This one and the stitches that accompany are not entirely new; they draw on the experience you have already.

The quickest and most straightforward way to learn any unique stitch is never, to begin with, a foundation chain but to add the new stitches in current stitches. For this, we'll start with a swatch.

Making a Half Double Crochet Stitches:

1. Begin with a foundation chain of eleven stitches. Add two single crochet lines (10 stitches per row).

2. Double half crochet stitches are 1.5 times the size of a single crochet stitch, and so you require two turning chains before starting each line of double half crochet stitches. Chain 2 and switch to start a new row.

3. The double half crochet stitch has an additional step: You have to yarn over when you start your stitch. So, wrap over and put the hook into your first stitch
(the same first, you'd picked if doing a single crochet).

4. Yarn over it again, and make a circle. You now have a total of 3 loops on your hook.

6. Yarn over it one more time and draw through these three loops: Now double half crochet is done!

COMPLETE THIS 1ST ROW by redoing steps 3 to 5 for every stitch, stitch across now chain two and turn your handy work over. You will note that with a single crochet, these stitches appear changed than what you've been used to see. Upon 1st view, the two threads at the top of your stitch seem to be facing you, the ones which appear like a cord (see image below).

Do not be delusional! The lower thread of the same chain approaching you is from the fresh yarn on which you operated at the start of the stitch, and the top thread was the front face loop at the top end of your stitch. When you tilt the item towards you, you'll notice that there are already two threads at the top edge of the thread, bent somewhat outward from yourself. You're going to be operating on the top two branches. Exercise this stitch for several rows only to get the pace

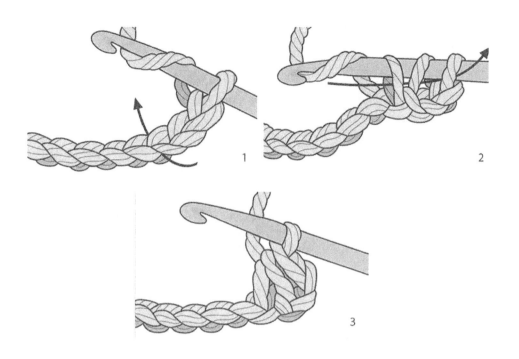

ANALYZING HALF DOUBLE Crochet

Since you've completed a couple of lines of half a double crochet stitches, let us see through them. Please remember that just like for a single crochet stitch, you see alternating lines of stitches on the top and bottom sides. A glance at the row that you have just finished, by holding your hook at the upper left corner (so you realize you're having a look at the right-hand side of those stitches), you now see the 2 strings that appear like a chain at the top of your stitch. Under those, 3 threads tend to follow each other around to form a triangle.

You would also note that after you slide your hook beneath the stitch's upper two strings, there is a 3rd strand below the vertical part of the stitches currently under the hook. Now see at two lines underneath that to see another section of rows on the right side that has a complete row of stitches going into it. The top chain is missing here, so you can easily see your triangle.

NOW, TURN THE WORK over, hold the hook in the top right-hand corner, and peek at the bottom side of the stitch. There's the fabricated "chain" the forms the top half of your stitch, and then you may also see two threads forming a V, very close to what a single crochet stitch appears on the upper side. Look down two rows under that to identify another section on the opposite side, which has a section of stitches working in it. The chain has also been shortened to only the lower part of your strand, with the V even now intact underneath, providing you a tad bit of a jagged ridge across the upper row.

TOP TIP: ONCE A CROCHET stitch has been finished, the front side of the stitch (the 2 chains like threads to which you attach the next row) is directly just to the right side of your stitch's post (the perpendicular section). This one is valid for every pattern. It's challenging to identify in the single crochet stitch because it is almost the section of the old stitch. Still, it's better to identify as the stitch becomes more significant, that is, with the double and treble crochet stitches discussed later on.

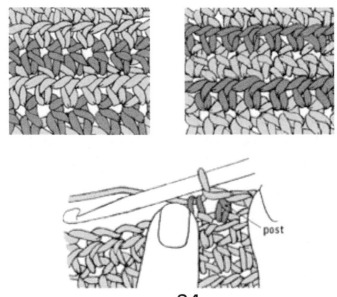

post

34

WORKING HALF DOUBLE Crochet into a Foundation Chain:

1.Begin with a piece that's not too large: a training swatch may be 10-half double crochet stitches broad is an ideal one.

2.Create 12 chains long to your foundation chain. (For a swatch of the size mentioned above, you will need 2 turning chains, so that our base chain should be 12 chains long: 10 + 2 = 12.)

3.Start counting back from the hook on your foundation chain (remember never to count the hook loop) to the third chain from your hook. This is the chain on which you'll create your first half double crochet stitch; for this first line, the 2 chains you decided to skip were your turning chains.

4-6. Redo steps 3-5 from the double half crochet stitch (DHCS) done before. To create the double half crochet stitch across the baseline, put your hook below the top strand of the next chain to continue each thread. Work your way through until you have a total of 10 double half crochets. You might want to practice several times the baseline, and this row.

Double Crochet

Double crochet stitches are an extra half stitch wider than double half crochet stitches, which are usually double the size of single crochet stitches. Thus, you do require 2 turning chains before starting each new row of stitches. You don't just yarn over before you start your stitch, but there's also an additional yarn over to complete it off. Begin by inserting the latest stitch into old stitches once more.

Working Double Crochet

1.Start a practicing swatch: construct an 11-stitch long foundation chain, instead 2 columns of single crochet (10 stitches per row) into this one.

2.Chain 2 (turning chains) and flip over the project to start the fresh row.

35

3.Yarn over and put the hook into your 1st stitch (the very same stitch you'd use in case of making single crochet).

4.Yarn over and over, and make a circle. You now have 3 loops on the crochet hook.

5.Yarn over again and pull it through two of the loops; you are left with two loops on to your hook.

1. Yarn over again and draw along the left of the two loops: This completes your double crochet.

2. Complete this 1st column of your double crochet, chain 2, and flip over the piece.

ONCE YOU FLIP OVER the work, you will find that all these double crochet stitches appear entirely different than what you used to see for a single or a half double crochet stitches. Now, in the upper section of the stitch, you'll identify what appears like a chain, except in this case, with an additional string looping beneath and between each of your "chain." The lower section of your stitch appears like two opposing circles stuck in one another, so there's the similar V we've seen in the half double crochet pattern.

Among these stitches, there will be wide-open spaces, so that it would be too easy to slide your hook through them and call it a day, but don't get tempted in by the space siren song. You must work just under the upper 2 lines. Exercise this stitch to have the flow of it for a couple more columns.

ANALYZING DOUBLE CROCHET

Since now you've completed a couple of rows of double crochet stitches, let's have a peek. Note that you may look at contrasting patterns on the top and bottom sides of the stitches much as for prior stitches.

• See the row you've just finished, with your hook at the upper left edge (so you recognize you're gazing at the right-hand side of those stitches). You will see the 2 strings that appear like a chain at the very top of your stitch, and beneath those, you'll find 2 strands that make up a V. This V ends in the very same 3 strands that tend to follow one another to form a triangle we've seen in the double half crochet stitch (A).

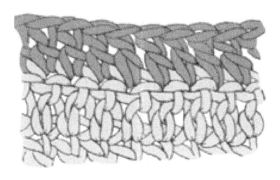

• Look down 2 rows beneath that to identify another section on the right that has a column of stitches working in it. The chain from the top is lacking, and you may still see the 2 strands forming a V, which end in the very same 3 strands forming a triangle (B).

• Then turn the bit over, in the top right corner with the pin, and aim at the opposite side of your stitches. Here you may notice what looks like a chain in the upper half with the additional string looping beneath and in between every "chain." The lower half of your stitch has almost the opposite face parenthesis and the identical V we saw with the double half crochet pattern.

• Look down 2 rows under that to identify another section on the opposite side, which has a column of stitches embedded in it. The "chain" has also been shortened to only the bottom strand and your 3rd strand between your chains, showing everyone a double dotted line with the parentheses and V still attached underneath.

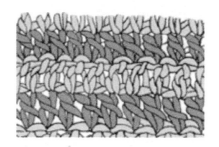

WORKING DOUBLE CROCHET into a Foundation Chain

1. Practice swatching 10 large double crochet stitches continue by creating a foundation chain of 12 chains long. (Note that you will need a 2-chain turning chain for a swatch this broad, so your foundation chain or base chain will be of 12 chains long)

2. Start counting back from the hook up to your hooks 3rd row. (Note never to add the hook loop in your counting.) Here is when you'll create the 1st double crochet stitch; the two chains that you've missed are turning chains for your 1st row.

3. Follow instructions to create a series of double crochet stitches defined in the section of the double crochet stitch. Keep going this way, putting your hook underneath the next chain's upper strand and finishing a double crochet stitch, respectively. Make your way, though, till 10 double crochets have been done. Exercise a few times the sequence of foundations, and this 1st column.

Treble Crochet

Treble crochet stitches, also referred to as triple crochet stitches, are two complete chains longer than a single crochet stitch, so we'll need a total of three turning chains before we start stitch each row. The treble stitch also has 2 additional steps: You yarn two times before you start your stitch, and there's an additional yarn over to complete it. Putting this latest stitch onto previous stitches, let's exercise as usual.

Working Treble Crochet

1. Create a foundation chain of eleven for your practicing swatch, and then create 2 single crochet rows into it (10 stitches per row).
2. Chain 3 and turn the project around to start the latest row.
3. Yarn over two times and put your hook into the 1st stitch (the same 1st stitch you should have selected for other stitches).
4. Yarn over again, and make a circle. You now have at your hook a total of 4 loops.
5. Yarn over again and pull through two of the loops on your hook; that leaves three circles on to your hook.
6. Repeat step 5: Yarn over your hook and pull out just 2 of the loops; that leave two loops on your hook
7. Yarn over repeatedly, and pull through the remaining 2 loops: full treble crochet. Complete this first row, Chain 3 and turn over the project.

ANALYZING TREBLE CROCHET

Since now a couple of rows of treble crochet stitches have been finished, let's take a closer look at these. Please remember that you'll see repeated rows on the right-hand side and the bottom side of the stitches, just as in past stitches.

• Look at the row you've just done, with the hook at the upper-left edge, and you recognize you're focusing at this row's right hand. You would see the 2 strands that appear like a chain at the top corner of the thread, and underneath those, you may see 2 strands that shape a V that ends in the same 3 strands that appear to chase one another in a triangle (A).

• That is what we noticed with the same three-strand triangle in a double crochet stitch). Look down 2 rows beneath that to identify another section on the right that has a line of stitches working inside of it. The chain at the top edge is absent, but the remainder of the thread is just the same: the 2 packed triangles and a V (B).

• Now turn over your piece, hook in the top right corner and peek at the bottom side of the stitches. Here you will notice what looks like a thread in the top half with the extra string looping below and between each "chain." There are 2 sets of parentheses in the bottom half of the stitch, and then there is the V (C).

• Look down two rows beneath that to identify another section on the opposite side which has a line of stitches operating in it. The "bar" has been shortened to the base of your strand, and the 3rd strand between both the chains offers you a double dotted line with parentheses couples, and the V stays unchanged below (D)

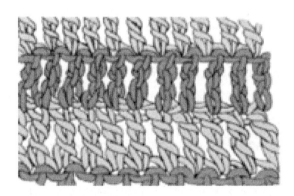

WORKING TREBLE CROCHET in a Set of Foundations

1.Begin with a 10 treble crochet stitches broad, swatch for practicing. The turning chain is chain no 3, so the foundation chain should be 13 chains long: 10 + 3 = 13.

2.Start counting from the hook to the fourth chain on your

hook on to your foundation chain. (Keep in mind, the hook loop doesn't count.) That's the chain where you'll create your 1st treble crochet stitch; the three chains you've missed are your turning chains for 1st row.

3.Replicate all the stages from the treble crochet stitch to make a treble crochet. Keep going this way, putting the hook underneath the next chain's upper strand and then doing a treble crochet stitch (TCS). Work your way through, before 10 treble crochets have been done. Perform a couple times more this chain of base stitch, and just this column

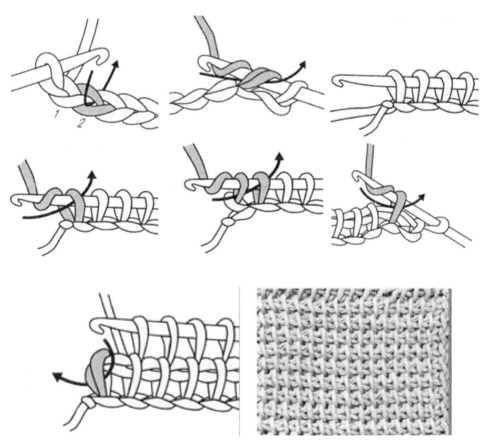

1.2 Knitting v/s Crochet

Needles v/s hook:

Pointed knitting needles, looms, or machines are used to produce knitting.

Looms and machines are used in large part for mass-production of products such as knitted products for the textile industry. You'll use a set of pointed knitting needles of copper, plastic, or wood while knitting by hand. Knitting needles of various projects can come in different sizes. Often, a string connects the twin needles, named as circular knitting.

Knitting needles can come in a pack of more than two as well. Double-pointed sock knitting needles, for instance, often sold in packs of four or five. Crocheters make small pieces by using a single crochet needle. A hook, which is a stick with a short hooked end, comes from small to big in all sizes. Usually, they're make of titanium, iron, bamboo, rubber, wood, or bone. Stitches: The substantial variations among the crocheted item and knitted items are significant. You'll have to hold multiple working yarn loops firmly on your needles for knitting. Each stitch is based on the stitch support underneath it. If a knitter loses one stitch, it will undo the whole row of stitches underneath it.

There's usually just one working yarn loop for conventional Crochet that requires care. Various circles require care, with specific specialized crochet crafts and niches, such as broomstick lace. The single active chain is what is holding together all the design and preventing it from untangling.

Projects: The knitting process with needles makes more polished fabric drape, which is why clothing is normally kneaded. Crochet makes soft, but somewhat tougher cloth, suitable for, for example, blankets and table runners. Today, though, there is such a huge array of yarns that makes it easy to construct intricate knits or crochet drapes. Based of your choice, you'll even come into items which can be knit and crocheted.

Chapter 4

CROCHET KITCHEN ITEMS

Having beautiful kitchen
items in your kitchen give a pleasing effect to the eyes. With the help of crochet you can make a plethora of items. Some of these are explained below

Blooming Flower Coaster Set

A beautiful flower is this duo's highlight, one circular and the other is square. The coasters would be a pleasant present to the hostess, and each ball of yarn would create four coasters.
Finished Measurements:
Square coaster: 3 " (9.5 cm) square.
Round coaster: 3 " (9 cm) in diameter

Square Coaster:
1. Chain 6, connects using a slip stitch (ss) to form a circle
2. Round 1 (Right Side): chain 1, 12 single crochet (sc) in the loop, connect using a slip stitch (ss) to your 1st.
3. Round 2: chain 3 (counts as double crochet (DC)), double crochet (DC)with in the very same stitch, two double crochet (DC)in every single crochet (sc) across, join using a slip stitch (ss) to the top of chain -3. Now you've got 24 double crochet (DC).
4. Round 3: chain 1, single crochet (sc) between next two double crochet (DC) posts, chain 3, skip the next three double crochet (DC), * single crochet (sc) from the space between last double crochet (DC) skipped and next double crochet (DC), chain 3, skip next three double crochet (DC); repeat from * six further times, enter using a slip stitch (ss) on first single crochet (sc).

44

You now have eight single crochet (sc) and eight chains -3 spaces.

5. Round 4: chain 1, single crochet (sc) in the very same single crochet (sc), * (half double crochet (hdc) (DC), double crochet (DC), three treble crochet (TC) (TC), double crochet (DC), half double crochet (hdc)) in next space * *, single crochet (sc) in next single crochet (sc); repeat from * around, end with the last repeat at * *, enter using slip stitch (ss) to single crochet (sc). You have eight petals in it now.

6. ROUND 5: chain 6 (counts as double crochet (DC), chain 3), * single crochet (sc) in center treble crochet (TC) of next petal, chain 3, * * double crochet (DC)in next single crochet (sc), chain 3, repeat from * through, end last repeat at * *, connect using slip stitch (ss) to 3rd chain of chain -6.

7.Round 6: Slip stitch (SS) into next chain -3 space, chain 1, 4 single crochet (sc) in the very same area, * five single crochet (sc) in next chain -3 space *, four single crochet (sc) in next chain -3 space, repeat from * circle, end last repeat at * *, enter using slip stitch (ss) to first single crochet (sc). Now you've got 72 single crochet (sc).

8.ROUND 7: chain 1, single crochet (sc) in the very same stitch, * single crochet (sc) in next three stitches, half double crochet (hdc)in next three stitches, dc in next two stitches, 3 stitches in next stitch, dc in next two stitches, half double crochet (hdc)in next three stitches, single crochet (sc) in next four stitches; repeat from * across, skip last single crochet (sc), enter with slip stitch (ss) in first single crochet (sc). Quick off. You've got 20 stitches to each side now. In the end, weave.

ROUND COASTER:
1. Operate till Rnd 6, just like with Square Coaster.
2. Round 7: Chain 1, single crochet (sc) in the very same stitch, .

then enter using slip stitch (ss) to beginning single crochet (sc) in every remaining stitch around. Fasten off. Weave in the ends

GOLDEN RAY OF SUNSHINE TRIVET

This small trivet is composed of two simple hexagonal patterns that are crocheted around each other. It can be seen in a single color here, yet color variations could add a bit of pizzazz on different rounds.

Finished Measurements: 6 inches (15 cm) in diameter at its widest points

Pattern Essentials:

Beg shell: (chain 3, double crochet (DC), chain 2, two double crochet (DC)) in the very same space.

Shell: (two double crochet (DC), chain 2, two double crochet (DC)) in the very same space.

Tight picot-3: chain 3, slip stitch (ss) to top of double crochet (DC) at base of the chain.

Picot shell: (3 double crochet (DC), tight picot-3, two double crochet (DC)) in the very same space.

Crocheting the Patterns (make 2)

1. Lightly chain 6, join to form a ring using a slip stitch (ss).

2. Round 1 (right side): chain 3 (throughout acts as a double crochet (DC)), three double crochet (DC)in a circle, chain 2, * four double crochet (DC)in a circle, chain 2; repeat from * four additional cycles, enter using slip stitch (ss) to top of chain -3, chain 1, transform. Now you have 24 double crochet (DC) and six chain -spaces.

3. Round 2 (wrong side): Slip stitch (SS) into chain -2 space, begin shell in the very same area, chain 2, * shell in the next space, chain 2; repeat from * four additional times, enter using slip stitch (ss) to top chain -3, chain 1, transform. Now you've

46

got six shells.

4. Round 3 (right side): Do not switch the pattern while you are focusing on the remaining stages. Slip stitch (SS) into chain -2 space, chain 3 (acts as double crochet (DC)), three double crochet (DC) in the very same space, chain 1, shell into next shell space, chain 1, * four double crochet (DC) in next space, chain 1, shell in next shell space, chain 1; repeat from * four more times, enter using slip stitch (ss) to top of chain- 3.

5. ROUND 4: Chain 3 (counts as double crochet (DC)), double crochet (DC) in next three double crochet (DC), * double crochet (DC) in next space, chain 1, shell in next shell space, chain 1, dc in next space * *, double crochet (DC) in next four double crochet (DC); repeat from * to, end last repeat at * *, enter using slip stitch (ss) to top chain -3.

6. ROUND 5: Chain 3 (counts as double crochet (DC)), double crochet (DC)in next four double crochet (DC), * double crochet (DC)in next space, chain 1, shell in next shell space, chain 1, double crochet (DC)in next space * *, double crochet (DC)in next six double crochet (DC); repeat from * around, end last repeat at * *, double crochet (DC)in next double crochet (DC), enter using slip stitch (ss) to top of chain-3.

7. ROUND 6: Chain 3 (counts as double crochet (DC)), double crochet (DC)in next five double crochet (DC), * double crochet (DC)in next space, chain 1, shell in next shell space, chain 1, double crochet (DC)in next space * *, double crochet (DC)in next eight double crochet (DC); repeat from * to, end last repeat at * *, double crochet (DC)in last two double crochet (DC), enter using slip stitch (ss) to top of chain-3.

1. ROUND 7: Chain 3 (counts as double crochet (DC)), double crochet (DC)in next six double crochet (DC), * double crochet

(DC)in next space, chain 1, shell in next shell space, chain 1, double crochet (DC)in next space * *, double crochet (DC)in next ten double crochet (DC); repeat from * to, end last repeat at * *, double crochet (DC)in last three double crochet (DC), enter using slip stitch (ss) to top of chain-3.

2. ROUND 8: Chain 3 (counts as double crochet (DC)), double crochet (DC)in next seven double crochet (DC), * double crochet (DC)in next space, chain 1, shell in next shell space, chain 1, double crochet (DC)in next space * *, double crochet (DC)in next 1two double crochet (DC); repeat from * around, end last repeat at * *, double crochet (DC)in last four double crochet (DC), enter using slip stitch (ss) to top of chain-3.

3. ROUND 9: Chain 3 (counts as double crochet (DC)), double crochet (DC)in next eight double crochet (DC), * double crochet (DC)in next space, chain 1, shell in next shell space, chain 1, double crochet (DC)in next space * *, double crochet (DC)in next 14 double crochet (DC); repeat from * to, end last repeat at * *, double crochet (DC)in last five double crochet (DC), enter using slip stitch (ss) to top of chain-3.

4. ROUND 10: Chain 3 (counts as double crochet (DC)), double crochet (DC)in next nine double crochet (DC), * double crochet (DC)in next space, chain 1, shell in next shell, chain 1, double crochet (DC)in next space * *, double crochet (DC)in next 16 double crochet (DC); repeat from * through, end last repeat at * *, double crochet (DC)in last six double crochet (DC), enter using slip stitch (ss) to top of chain-3.

5. Fasten off. In the end, weave.

Joining the Motifs

1. Facing the wrong side, line up and edges suit. Enter thread with slip stitch (ss) in chain-1 space before any shell, ensuring all patterns are crocheted here and throughout. Chain 3 (counts as

double crochet (DC)), (two double crochet (DC), close picot-3, two double crochet (DC)) in the very same space — begin picot shell made, * picot shell in next shell space, picot shell in next chain-1 space, (skip next three double crochet (DC), picot shell between 3rd and 4th double crochet (DC)) 5 times, picot shell in next chain-1 space; repeat from * around, remove the last picot shell, join using slip stitch (ss) to top of chain-3. Do not fasten off. You now have 48 shells to picot.

Creating the Hanging Loop (optional)

1. Foundation single crochet (sc) 18. Skip two picot shells from next. Slip stitch (ss) of the next picot shell into last double crochet (DC). Fasten in the ends and weave in

Tunisian Pot Holders

These potholders are crafted in plain Tunisian stitch, which creates a woven-looking pattern, almost too beautiful to use in a kitchen. When working with a solid or striped yarn, they look lovely and are double-layered for additional protection.

Finished Measurements: Approximately 7 inch × 7 1/2 inch (18 × 19 cm)

Gauge: 14 stitches & 14 rows = 4 inches (10 cm) in pattern on an afghan hook

Crocheting the Pot Holder

1. Using an Afghan hook, chain 24.

2. Working even using Tunisian Simple Stitch (TSS), for the next 20 rows, stop at a returning row. Now change to a smaller size crochet hook.

3. Chain 1 (counts as first stitch), slip stitch (ss) in each vertical strip across, work down the side edge, slip stitch (ss) in every row end strand across, work across the bottom edge, slip stitch (ss) in every chain across, work down the side edge, slip stitch (ss) in each row end stitch across to starting, slip stitch (ss) in

first slip stitch. You now got a total of 88 slip stitches.

4.Fasten off and, in the end, weave in.

Joining the Two Sides

1.Keep the pieces together with the wrong sides facing.

2.Leaving a 30 inch (76 cm) tail for your hanging loop, connect yarn using slip stitch (ss) in the upper right side corner; work by double thickness in the front loops only for the front piece and front loops only of the back piece, chain 1, * three single crochet (sc) in corner stitch, single crochet (sc) in each stitch to the next corner; redo from * around, connect using slip stitch (ss) in first single crochet (sc). Don't fasten off yet.

Making The Hanging Loop

•Hold your working yarn and the long tail that you left at the start together, chain 14; join using slip stitch to first single crochet (sc) to create a loop.

Chapter 5

CROCHET PERSONAL ITEMS

Crochet Mittens

Make the ribbing:
- Row 1. Using size G hook and main color yarn, Ch 7 (9, 11) sts. Make 1 sc st into the back bump of the 2nd ch from hook, make 1 sc st into the remaining 5 (7, 9) sts. 6 (8, 10) sts.
- Row 2. Turn, ch 1 (this is a turning chain, do not count as a stitch), 1 sc tbl into each st across. 6 (8, 10) sets
- Rows 3 through rows 21 (27, 31): Repeat row 2, 19 (25, 29) more times. 6 (8, 10) sts in each row, 21 (27, 31) rows worked, not including the foundation chain).

Hold the ribbing so that your crochet hook is at the right side of your work (as though you are about to work another row). Take the beginning edge of your ribbing (the foundation chain edge) and bring it in front of the last row that you worked. In

51

other words, fold the ribbing in half and line up the short edges. Your crochet hook will be to the right, and in the row behind the beginning yarn tail. Slip stitch these rows together by inserting your hook into the back loop of the foundation chain and then through the back loop of the stitch directly behind it (from the last row worked), yo and pull loop through to front of work and through loop on hook. Repeat across row. 6 (8, 10) sl sts worked. Do not fasten off! Turn ribbing tube so that the sl st row is to the inside. (The sl st row is on the wrong side of the cuff.) You will now stitch into the edges of the previous rows.

Make the body of each mitten:

- Round 1. Make 23 (28, 33) sc sts, equally spaced, around top edge of ribbing. (23, 28, 33 sts).

- Round 2. 1 sc into each of the next 10 (12, 15) sts, 2 sc into the next st, 1 sc into each of the next 2 sts, 2 sc into the next st, 1 sc into each of the next 9 (12, 14) sts. 25 (30, 35) sts.

- Round 3. 1 sc into each st around. 25 (30, 35) sts.

- Round 4. 1 sc into each of the next 11 (13, 16) sts, 2 sc into the next st, 1 sc into each of the next 2 sts, 2 sc into the next st, 1 sc into each of the next 10 (13, 15) sts. 27 (32, 37) sts

- Round 5. 1 sc into each st around. 27 (32, 37) sts.

- Round 6. 1 sc into each of the next 12 (14, 17) sts, 2 sc into the next st, 1 sc into each of the next 2 sts, 2 sc into the next st, 1 sc into each of the next 11 (14, 16) sts. 29 (34, 39) sts.

- Round 7. 1 sc into each st around. 29 (34, 39) sts.

- Round 8. 1 sc into each of the next 13 (15, 18) sts, 2 sc into the next st, 1 sc into each of the next 2 sts, 2 sc into the next st, 1 sc into each of the next 12 (15, 17) sts. 31 (36, 41) sts.
- Round 9. 1 sc into each st around. 31 (36, 41) sts.
- Round 10. 1 sc into each of the next 14 (16, 19) sts, 2 sc into the next st, 1 sc into each of the next 2 sts, 2 sc into the next st, 1 sc into each of the next 13 (16, 18) sts. 33 (38, 43) sts.

For Preschool size only: skip to round 16 after completing this round.

- Round 11. 1 sc into each st around. (Older kids-38, Women-43) sts.
- Round 12. 1 sc into each of the next (17, 20) sts, 2 sc into the next st, 1 sc into each of the next 2 sts, 2 sc into the next st, 1 sc into each of the next (17, 19) sts. (Older kids-40, Women-45 sts).
- Round 13. 1 sc into each st around. (Older kids-40, Women-45 sts).

For older kids size only: skip to round 16 after completing this round.

- Round 14. 1 sc into each of the next 21 sts, 2 sc into the next st, 1 sc into each of the next 2 sts, 2 sc into the next st, 1 sc into each of the next 20 sts (Women-47 sts).
- Round 15. 1 sc into each st around (Women-47 sts).
- Round 16. 1 sc into each of the next 12 (14, 17) sts, skip the next 10 (12, 14) sts (for thumb), 1 sc into each of the next 11 (14, 16) sts. 23 (28, 33) sts around hand, not including thumb.
- Round 17. 1 sc into each st around. 23 (28, 33) sts.

Repeat round 17 until the measurement from the thumbhole, up, is 2 (2 3/4″, 3 1/2″). [Approximately 9 (12, 15) more rounds]

- For Preschool Size only: Next round: [1 sc into each of the next 6 sts, sctog] 2 times, 1 sc into each of the next 5 sts, sc2tog (20 sts). Next round: [1 sc into each of the next 3 sts, sc2tog] 4 times (16 sts). Next round: 1 sc into each st around (16 sts). Next round: sc2tog 8 times (8 sts).Fasten off with a 10″ tail. Using yarn needle, thread yarn tail through the front loop of the remaining 8 sts and pull tight. Weave in ends.

- For Older Kid Size only: Next round: [1 sc into each of the next 5 sts, sc2tog] 4 times (24 sts). Next round: 1 sc into each st around (24 sts). Next round: sc2tog 12 times (12 sts). Next round: 1 sc into each st around (12 sts). Next round: [1 sc into the next st, sc2tog] 4 times (8 sts).Fasten off with a 10″ tail. Using yarn needle, thread yarn tail through the front loop of the remaining 8 sts and pull tight. Weave in ends.

- For Women's Size only: Next round: [1 sc into each of the next 9 sts, sc2tog] 3 times (30 sts). Next round: 1 sc in each st around (30 sts). Next round: [1 sc into each of the next 3 sts, sc2tog] 6 times (24 sts). Next round: 1 sc into each st around (24 sts). Next round: sc2tog 12 times (12 sts). Next round: 1 sc into each st (12 sts). Next round: [1 sc into the next st, sc2tog] 4 times (8 sts). Fasten off with a 10″ tail. Using yarn needle, thread yarn tail through the front loop of the remaining 8 sts and pull tight. Weave in ends.

Crochet Mittens Thumb:

Join yarn to any thumb stitch and make 10 (12, 14) sc stitches around. 1 sc into each st around until thumb measures 1 1/2″ (2″, 2 1/2″) from crotch (about 5, 7, 9 more rows).

Next row: sc2tog 5 (6, 7) times (5, 6, 7 sts left). Fasten off with a 10″ tail. Using yarn needle, thread yarn tail through the front loop of the remaining 5 (6, 7) sts and pull tight. Weave in ends.

Optional Star Appliqué:
- Round 1. Make a magic ring, 5 sc into ring, pull on beginning yarn tail to tighten ring. (5 sts)

- Round 2. 2 sc into each stitch around. (10 sts)

- Round 3. [Chain 4, 1 sc into the back bump of the second chain from the hook, 1 hdc into the back bump of the next chain, 1 dc into the back bump of the next chain, skip the next stitch from round 2, 1 slip st into next st] 5 times. Fasten off with long yarn tail. Use this yarn tail to stitch the star onto the mitten.

Crochet Eyeglass Holder Pattern

CROCHET STITCHES + ABBREVIATIONS

ch = chain
st(s)= stitch(es)
hdc(s) = half double crochet(s)
sk = skip
rep = repeat
hdc inc = half double crochet increase (2 hdcs in the same st)

The Eyeglass Case Pattern Steps
Foundation Row: ch 21

- Row 1: in 3rd ch from hook hdc, *sk 1 ch, hdc increase in next ch, rep from * ending with hdc increase in last ch, turn. (19)
- Row 2: Ch 2, in first st hdc, *sk 1 st, hdc increase in next st, rep from * ending with a hdc increase in last st, turn. ch 2.
- Row 3-12: Rep row 2
- Row 13: Ch 1, sc in first st, *sl st in next, sc in next st rep from * for a total of 7 sts, sk 1 st, ch 3, **sl st in next st, sc in next st, rep from ** for a total of 7 sts ending with a sc in the last st, fasten off. You will end with a st count of (18)

Finishing: Fold up the bottom of the case as shown in the picture above, or about 2.5″.
Cut two 6″ pieces of yarn and sew together the sides of the case with a yarn needle. You can use a whip stitch to join if you'd prefer.
Attach the button to the center of the case.
Weave in loose ends throughout the case.

Crochet Shawl Granny Pattern

Row 1: Start with a ch 3, in the 3rd ch from the hook dc 2 times, ch 2, dc 3 times in the same stitch, turn. (6)

Row 2: ch 3, 2 dc in first st, sk 2 st's and ch 1, dc 3 times in the ch 2 space from the row before, ch 2, dc 3 more times in the same ch 2 space, ch 1, sk 2 sts, end with 3 dc's in the last st, turn. (12)

Row 3: ch 3, dc 2 times in the first st, ch 1, dc 3 times in the next ch 1 space, ch 1, dc 3 times in the next ch 2 space, ch 2, dc 3 times in the same ch 2 space, ch 1, dc 3 times in the next ch 1 space, ch 1, sk 2 sts, dc 3 times into the last st, turn. (18)

Row 4: ch 3, dc 2 times in the first st, ch 1, dc 3 times in the next ch 1 space, ch 1, dc 3 times in the next ch 1 space, ch 1, dc 3 times in the next ch 2 space, ch 2, dc 3 times in the same ch 2 space, ch 1, dc 3 times int the next ch 1 space, ch 1, dc 3 times in the next ch 1 space, ch 1, sk 2 sts, end with 3 dc's in last st, turn. (24)

Row 5 – 32: Repeat row 4. The stitch counts for each row will be as follows starting with Row 5 and ending with row 32.
Stitch Count for Rows 5- 32: 30,36,42,48,54,60, 66,72,78,84,90,96,102, 108,114,120,126, 132,138,144,150,156, 162,168,174,180,186, 192

Crochet a Tote Bag

- Round 1: Starting with Color A ch 3, 10 dc In 3rd ch from hook, sl to the first dc. (10)
- Round 2: Ch 3, in first st dc, ch 1, * dc, ch 1 rep around from *, sl st to first dc. (chain 1's count as a st here and throughout the pattern) (20)
- Round 3: Ch 3, dc, 2 dc in ch 1 space, * dc on top of dc from previous round, 2 dc in ch 1 space, rep around from *, sl st to first dc. (30)
- Round 4: Ch 3, dc, ch 1, * dc, ch 1 rep around from *, sl st to first dc. (60)
- Round 5: Ch 3, *dc, 1 dc in ch 1 space, dc, 2 dc in ch 1 space, rep from * around, sl st to top of first dc. (75)

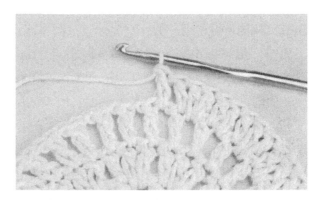

- Round 6: Ch 3, * Ch 1, sk 1 st, dc in next st, repeat from * around, ending with a ch 1 and sk st, sl st to top of first ch 1, (76)
- After this round the purse should start to take shape since there are no more increase rounds.
- Round 7: Ch 3, 2 dc in every ch 1 space around, sl st to first Dc (76)
- Round 8: Ch 3, * Ch 1, sk 1 st, dc in next st, repeat from * around, sl st to top of first ch 1, (76)

- Round 9: Repeat round 7 (76)
- Round 10: Repeat round 8 (76)
- Round 11: Repeat round 7 (76)
- Round 12: Repeat round 8 (76)
- Round 13: Repeat round 7 (76)
- Round 14: Repeat round 8 (76)
- Round 15: Repeat round 7 (76)
- Round 16: Repeat round 8 (76)
- Round 17: Repeat round 7 (76)
- Round 18: Repeat round 8 (76)
- Round 19: Change color to Jute, ch 1, *2 sc in ch 1 space, repeat from * around (76)
- Round 20: ch 1, sc in every st, sl st to the top of the first st (76)
- Round 21: Repeat round 20(76)
- Round 22: Repeat round 20 (76)
- Round 23: Repeat round 20 (76)

Making the Handles

Make sure you crochet up two handles. Each handle should measure approximately 24 inches (61 cm) long. Note that it will stretch as it is used, so be mindful of that.

Row 1: Ch 6, sc in 2nd ch from hook and every ch across, turn (5)

Row 2: Ch 1, sc in every ch across (5)

Row 3-60: Repeat row 2 (5)

Half Double Crochets Infinity Scarf

With Color A Ch 126

Row 1: In the second ch from the hook hdc, hdc into each ch across, turn. (125)

Row 2: Ch 1, hdc into the bl of the first st, hdc bl st into each st across, turn. (125)

Row 3 – 7 : Repeat row 2 for the rest of the pattern. (125)

Fasten off.

Finishing

Join two short ends together making sure rows line up and weave together using a whip stitch.

Chapter 6

CROCHET HOME DECOR ITEMS

Aura Wall Hanging

ABBREVIATIONS

Ch – chain
Sc – single crochet
Dc – double crochet
BLO – Back loop only
FLO – Front loop only
St(s) – Stitch(es)
Sk – Skip
RS – Right Side
WS – Wrong Side
Picot – See Special Stitch

Row 1 (WS) – In magic circle, ch 2 (doesn't count here and throughout) and work 7 dc. Pull tail tight. (7)
Row 2 (RS)- ch 2, turn. Place 2 dc BLO in each st. (14)
Row 3 (WS) – ch 2, turn. All in FLO, work [1 dc 1 st, 2 dc next st]. Repeat inside brackets 7x. (21)
Row 4 (RS) – ch 2, turn. All in BLO, work [1 dc 2 sts, 2 dc following st]. Repeat inside brackets 7x. (28)
Row 5 (WS) – ch 2, turn. All in FLO, work [1 dc 3 sts, 2 dc following st]. Repeat inside brackets 7x. (35)

Finish last st of R5 with CB.

Row 6 (RS) – ch 3 (counts as dc and ch 1), sk 1, dc BLO next. [ch 1, sk 1, dc BLO next]. Repeat inside brackets to end of row. (17 ch 1 spaces, 18 dc).

Finish last st of R6 with CA.

Row 7 (WS) – ch 2, turn. Work 1 dc same st, 2 dc in each of the next 2 ch spaces, 3 dc in each of the next 13 chain spaces, 2 dc in each of the next 2 ch spaces, 1 dc in 2nd ch of ch 3. (49)

Special Note: You might feel like Row 6 isn't staying straight on the sides, especially once Row 7 is complete. Because Row 6 is made of double crochets separated by chain 1 spaces, the double crochets at the start and end of the row don't stand up as straight for now. Don't worry, as you continue adding on rows, they will stand straight. We also add rows for edging on this straight edge, which will keep the edge straight.

Row 8 (RS) – ch 2, turn. All in BLO, work [1 dc 6 sts, 2 dc following st]. Repeat inside brackets 7x. (56)

Row 9 (WS) – ch 2, turn. All in FLO, work [1 dc 7 sts, 2 dc following st]. Repeat inside brackets 7x. (63)

Finish last st of R9 with CB.

Row 10 (RS) – ch 3 (counts as dc and ch 1), sk 1, dc BLO next. [ch 1, sk 1, dc BLO next]. Repeat inside brackets to end of row. (31 ch 1 spaces, 32 dc).

Finish last st of R10 with CA.

Row 11 (WS) – ch 2, turn. Work 1 dc same st, 2 dc in each of the next 3 ch spaces. [3 dc in next ch space, 2 dc in following ch space]. Repeat inside brackets 13x until 2 chain 1 spaces remain. In each space, work 2 dc. 1 dc in 2nd ch of ch 3. (77)

Row 12 (RS) – ch 2, turn. All in BLO, work [1 dc 10 sts, 2 dc following st]. Repeat inside brackets 7x. (84)

Do not finish off, we will do the edging of the straight line before finishing off.

Edging

With right side facing,

- Row 1 – ch 1 (doesn't count here or throughout), evenly place 48 sc across the raw straight edge. This means placing 2 sc in the side of each dc or ch 3. (48)
- Row 2 – ch 1, turn. Place 1 sc in each st across. (48)
- Finish last stitch of Row 2 with CB.
- Row 3 – ch 4 (counts 1 turning chain and as ch 3), turn. Sk 1st and 2nd st, sc next. [ch 3, sk 2 sts, sc next]. Repeat inside brackets across the row to end. (16 ch spaces)
- Finish last st of Row 3 with CA.
- Row 4 – ch 1, turn. In each ch space, work [3 sc, 1 picot, 2 sc] for a total of 5 sts in each space. (80 sc, picots don't count toward stitch count).

Boho Granny Stitch Crochet Garland

Abbreviations: US Terms

Ch – chain

Dc – Double Crochet

Sc – single crochet

Sl st – Slip Stitch

St – stitch

Sp – Space

Working into the ring: Work 3 dc. Ch 2. Work 3 dc. Turn. (8 sts)

2. Ch 2. Work 2 dc in same st. Ch 1. Working into next ch 2 sp: Work 3 dc. Ch 2. Work 3 dc.
Ch 1. Work 2 dc in last st. Turn. (14 sts)

3. Ch 2. Work 2 dc in same st. Ch 1. Work 3 dc in next ch 1 sp. Ch 1. Working into next ch 2 sp: Work 3 dc. Ch 2. Work 3 dc. Ch 1. Work 3 dc in next ch 1 sp. Ch 1. Work 2 dc in last st. Turn. (22 sts)

4. Ch 2. Work 2 dc in same st. Ch 1. *Work 3 dc in next ch 1 sp, Ch 1.* work twice.

Working into next ch 2 sp: Work 3 dc. Ch 2. Work 3 dc. Ch 1. *Work 3 dc in next ch 1 sp. Ch 1.* work twice. Work 2 dc in last st. Turn. (30 sts)

5. Ch 2. Work 2 dc in same st. Ch 1. *Work 3 dc in next ch 1 sp, Ch 1.* work 3 times.
Working into next ch 2 sp: Work 3 dc. Ch 2. Work 3 dc. Ch 1. *Work 3 dc in next ch 1 sp. Ch 1.* work three times. Work 2 dc in last st. Turn. (38 sts)

To create fringe, cut 8 lengths of yarn double the length of the length of the fringe you would like. Attach one piece in each of the space up and down the sides of each triangle. To do this, half your length, push the middle loop through the hole, then pull both end through the loop, pulling to tighten.

Add a fluffy tassel at the very bottom. Wrap yarn around a card about the width of the length you would like your finished tassel to be. Wrap 9 or 10 times. Cut the bottom, leaving the top loops uncut. Pull through the bottom ch space. Tie a shorter length of yarn around the middle, making the lengths into a tassel.
From here, you can sc each triangle together. Starting with one, join at the top right of the raw hypotenuse of the triangle. Sc across this raw edge as evenly as you can.

When you get to the end, grab your second triangle. Without breaking the yarn, and continuing to work as evenly as possible, sc into the first sp of the next triangle and continue sc across it. Repeat with all your triangles until they are all sewn together. String your crochet garland up to add some pretty to any place!

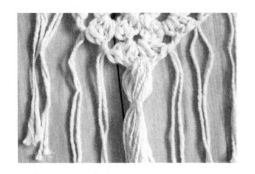 

Sunflower Pillow

Hand-colored Freia yarn makes in a single skein just one change from yellowish to green, brown, and crimson to dark purple. This pillow makes the most out of the whole yarn to taking advantage of the colorful design.

Finished Measurements: 12 inches (30.5 cm) square

Gauge: Rounds 1–6 = 3 3/4 inches (9.5 cm)

Pattern Essentials

Beg popcorn: Chain 3 (classifies as double crochet (DC)), make four additional double crochet (DC)in the same stitch, release the loop from your hook and push the hook from the front side to the back through the top edge of chain-3 through the removed loop and now pull through 2 loops on the hook.

Popcorn: Make five double crochet (DC) in 1 stitch, release the loop from your hook and push the hook from the front side to the back via the top of your first stitch in the popcorn, then into the released loop, yarn over and pull through 2 loops on the hook.

Crocheting the Pillow Front

1. Start with an adjustable ring.

2. Round 1: Chain 1, 12 single crochet (sc) in a circle, attach with slip stitch (ss) to your first single crochet (sc). Now you've got 12 single crochet (sc) .

3. Round 2: Chain 3 (counts as double crochet (DC) here and in all), double crochet (DC) in the same stitch, two double crochet (DC) in each single crochet (sc) around, connect with slip stitch (ss) to top of your chain-3. Now you've got 24 double crochet (DC).

4. Round 3: Chain 3, 2 double crochet (DC) in next double crochet (DC), * double crochet (DC) in next double crochet (DC), two double crochet (DC) in next double crochet (DC); repeat from * around, connect using slip stitch (ss) to top of chain-3. Now you've got 36 double crochet (DC).

5. Round 4: Beg popcorn in the first stitch, two single crochet (sc) in next double crochet (DC), * popcorn in next double crochet (DC), two single crochet (sc) in next double crochet (DC); repeat from * around, connect using slip stitch (ss) to top of beg popcorn. You have 54 sts in it now.

6. Round 5: Chain 1, starting in the first stitch, * single crochet (sc) in next eight sts, two single crochet (sc) in next stitch, repeat from * around, join using slip stitch (ss) to first single crochet (sc) . Now you've got 60 double crochet (DC).

7. Round 6: Chain 3, double crochet (DC) in each single crochet (sc) around, join with slip stitch (ss) to top of chain-3.

8. Round 7: Chain 1, single crochet (sc) in each double crochet (DC) around, connect with slip stitch (ss) to first single crochet (sc).

9.Round 8: Chain 2 (counts as front post double crochet (DC)), front post double crochet (DC) in next three single crochet (sc) , two front post double crochet (DC) in next single crochet (sc) , * front post double crochet (DC) in next four single crochet (sc) , two front post double crochet (DC) in next single crochet (sc) ; repeat from * around, join using slip stitch (ss) to top of chain-2. Now you've got 72 double crochet (DC).

10.Round 9: Chain 1, starting in the first stitch, * single crochet (sc) in next five sts, two single crochet (sc) in next stitch, repeat from * around, join with a slip stitch (ss) to first single crochet (sc). Now you've got 84 single crochet (sc).

11.Round 10: Chain 2 (counts as front post double crochet (DC)), front post double crochet (DC) in next 12 single crochet (sc) , two front post double crochet (DC) in next single crochet (sc) , * front post double crochet (DC) in next 13 single crochet (sc) , two front post double crochet (DC) in next single crochet (sc) ; redo from * around, join using slip stitch (ss) to top of chain-2. You have 90 sts on it now.

12.Round 11: Beg popcorn, single crochet (sc) in next stitch, two single crochet (sc) in next stitch, * popcorn in next stitch, single crochet (sc) in next stitch, single crochet (sc) in next stitch, two single crochet (sc) in next stitch; repeat from * around, join via slip stitch (ss) to top of beg popcorn. Now, you've got 120 sts.

13.Round 12: Chain 1, single crochet (sc) in every stitch around, connect with slip stitch (ss) to first single crochet (sc).

14.Round 13: Chain 2 (counts as half double crochet (HDC)), half double crochet (HDC) incoming eight single crochet (sc), two half double crochet (HDC) in next single crochet (sc), * * half double crochet (HDC) in next nine single crochet (sc), two half double crochet (HDC) in next single crochet (sc); redo from * around, attach using slip stitch (ss) to the top of chain-2.

Now you've got 132 half double crochet (HDC).

15.Round 14: Chain 3 (counts as double crochet (DC)), double crochet (DC) in next nine half double crochet (HDC), two double crochet (DC) in next half double crochet (HDC), * double crochet (DC) in next ten half double crochet (HDC), two double crochet (DC) in next half double crochet (HDC); repeat from * around, connect with slip stitch (ss) to top of chain-3.Now you've got 144 double crochet (DC).

16.Round 15: Chain 1, starting at first stitch, * single crochet (sc) at next 23 double crochet (DC), two single crochet (sc) at next double crochet (DC); repeat from * through, enter with slip stitch (ss) to first single crochet (sc). Now you've got 150 single crochet (sc).

17.Round 16: Chain 2, front post double crochet (DC), enter with slip stitch (ss) to top of chain-2 in every stitch around.

18.Round 17: Chain 3, double crochet (DC) in every stitch around, join with slip stitch (ss) to top of chain-2.

19.Round 18: Chain 1, single crochet (sc) in every stitch around, enter with slip stitch (ss) to first single crochet (sc).

20.Round 19: Chain 2 (counts as half double crochet (HDC)), half double crochet (HDC) in next 23 single crochet (sc), two half double crochet (HDC) in next single crochet (sc), * half double crochet (HDC) in next 24 single crochet (sc), two half double crochet (HDC) in next single crochet (sc); repeat from * around, join using slip stitch (ss) to top chain-2. You have 156 half double crochet (HDC) in it now.

21.Round 20: chain 1, single crochet (sc) in first six half double crochet (HDC), * half double crochet (HDC) in next six half double crochet (HDC), double crochet (DC) in next seven half double crochet (HDC), three treble crochet in next half double crochet (HDC), double crochet (DC) in next seven half double crochet (HDC), half double crochet (HDC) in next six half double crochet (HDC), single crochet (sc) in next 12 half double crochet (HDC); repeat from * around, skip last six single crochet (sc) , join using slip stitch (ss) in first single crochet (sc) . You have 164 sts in it now.

22.Round 21: Chain 1, single crochet (sc) in first six single crochet (sc) , * half double crochet (HDC) in next six half double crochet (HDC), double crochet (DC) in next seven double crochet (DC), treble crochet in next stitch, three treble crochet in next treble crochet, treble crochet in next treble crochet, double crochet (DC) in next seven double crochet (DC), half double crochet (HDC) in next six half double crochet (HDC), single crochet (sc) in next 12 single crochet (sc) ; repeat from * around, skip last six single crochet (sc) , connect with slip stitch (ss) to first single crochet (sc) . You have now 172 sts.

23.ROUND 22: chain 1, single crochet (sc) in first six single crochet (sc) , * half double crochet (HDC) in next six half double crochet (HDC), double crochet (DC) in next seven double crochet (DC), treble crochet in next two treble crochet, three treble crochet in next treble crochet, treble crochet in next two treble crochet, double crochet (DC) in next seven double crochet (DC), half double crochet (HDC) in next six half double crochet (HDC), single crochet (sc) in next 12 single crochet (sc) ; repeat from * around, omit last six single crochet (sc) , attach using slip stitch (ss) to 1st single crochet (sc) . You have 180 sts in it now.

24.Round 23: Chain 1, single crochet (sc) in first six single crochet (sc) , * half double crochet (HDC) in next six half double crochet (HDC), double crochet (DC) in next seven double crochet (DC), treble crochet in next three treble crochet, three treble crochet in next treble crochet, treble crochet in next three treble crochet, double crochet (DC) in next seven double crochet (DC), half double crochet (HDC) in next six half double crochet (HDC), single crochet (sc) in next 12 single crochet (sc) ; repeat from * around, skipping last six single crochet (sc) , connect with slip stitch (ss) to first single crochet (sc) . You have 188 sts in it now.

Round 24: chain 1, single crochet (sc) in first six single crochet (sc) , * half double crochet (HDC) in next six half double crochet (HDC), double crochet (DC) in next seven double crochet (DC), treble crochet in next four treble crochet, three treble crochet in next treble crochet, treble crochet in next four treble crochet, double crochet (DC) in next seven double crochet (DC), half double crochet (HDC) in next six half double crochet (HDC), single crochet (sc) in next 12 single crochet (sc) ; repeat from * around, omitting last six single crochet (sc) , attach using slip stitch (ss) to first single crochet (sc) . Now, you've got 196 sts.

Round 25: Chain 2 (counts as half double crochet (HDC)), half double crochet (HDC) in next 22 sts, two half double crochet (HDC) in next three sts, * half double crochet (HDC) in next 46 sts, two half double crochet (HDC) in next three sts; repeat from * twice more, half double crochet (HDC) in next 23 sts, attach using slip stitch (ss) to top chain-2. Fasten off. Block completed cover to 12 inches (30.5 cm) square.rochet; repeat from * around, skip last 6 single crochet (sc) , join using slip stitch (ss) in first single crochet (sc) . You have 164 sts in it now.

Round 21: Chain 1, single crochet (sc) in first 6 single crochet (sc) , * half double crochet (HDC) in next 6 half double crochet (HDC), double crochet (DC) in next 7 double crochet (DC), treble crochet in next stitch, 3 treble crochet in next treble crochet, treble crochet in next treble crochet, double crochet (DC) in next 7 double crochet (DC), half double crochet (HDC) in next 6 half double crochet (HDC), single crochet (sc) in next

12 single crochet (sc) ; repeat from * around, skip last 6 single crochet (sc) , connect with slip stitch (ss) to first single crochet (sc) . You have now 172 sts.

ROUND 22: chain 1, single crochet (sc) in first 6 single crochet (sc) , * half double crochet (HDC) in next 6 half double crochet (HDC), double crochet (DC) in next 7 double crochet (DC), treble crochet in next 2 treble crochet, 3 treble crochet in next treble crochet, treble crochet in next 2 treble crochet, double crochet (DC) in next 7 double crochet (DC), half double crochet (HDC) in next 6 half double crochet (HDC), single crochet (sc) in next 12 single crochet (sc) ; repeat from * around, omit last 6 single crochet (sc) , attach using slip stitch (ss) to 1st single crochet (sc) . You have 180 sts in it now.

Round 23: Chain 1, single crochet (sc) in first 6 single crochet (sc) , * half double crochet (HDC) in next 6 half double crochet (HDC), double crochet (DC) in next 7 double crochet (DC), treble crochet in next 3 treble crochet, 3 treble crochet in next treble crochet, treble crochet in next 3 treble crochet, double crochet (DC) in next 7 double crochet (DC), half double crochet (HDC) in next 6 half double crochet (HDC), single crochet (sc) in next 12 single crochet (sc) ; repeat from * around, skipping last 6 single crochet (sc) , connect with slip stitch (ss) to first single crochet (sc) . You have 188 sts in it now.

Round 24: chain 1, single crochet (sc) in first 6 single crochet (sc) , * half double crochet (HDC) in next 6 half double crochet (HDC), double crochet (DC) in next 7 double crochet (DC), treble crochet in next 4 treble crochet, 3 treble crochet in next treble crochet, treble crochet in next 4 treble crochet, double crochet (DC) in next 7 double crochet (DC), half double crochet (HDC) in next 6 half double crochet (HDC), single crochet (sc) in next 12 single crochet (sc) ; repeat from * around, omitting last 6 single crochet (sc) , attach using slip stitch (ss) to

72

first single crochet (sc) . Now, you've got 196 sts.

Round 25: Chain 2 (counts as half double crochet (HDC)), half double crochet (HDC) in next 22 sts, 2 half double crochet (HDC) in next 3 sts, * half double crochet (HDC) in next 46 sts, 2 half double crochet (HDC) in next 3 sts; repeat from * twice more, half double crochet (HDC) in next 23 sts, attach using slip stitch (ss) to top chain-2. Fasten off. Block completed cover to 12 inch (30.5 cm) square.

MAKING THE FABRIC PILLOW Back
• Fold and push a 1/2 inch (1.3 cm) fringe on all the sides of your cloth. Utilizing matching pearl cotton and sewing needle, embroider a series of chain stitches underneath the folding line along all four sides of the cloth pillow covering, working 52 chain stitches on every side. Chain stitches will be the same size as half double crochet (HDC) stitches in round 25 of the knit cover.

Joining Crochet to Fabric
• Round 1: Join the crocheted cover to the cloth pillow starting at the corner of one side as follows: Chain 1, single crochet (sc) via each half double crochet (HDC) and chain stitch around, connect using slip stitch (ss) to first single crochet (sc), add pillow before finishing the fourth line.
• Round 2: chain 1, * * (single crochet (sc) , picot-2, single crochet (sc) , picot-3, single crochet (sc) , picot-4, single crochet (sc) , picot-3, single crochet (sc) , picot-2, single crochet (sc)) in corner stitch, * chain 4, skip three sts, (single crochet (sc) , picot-4, single crochet (sc)) in next stitch; repeat from * across to 4 sts in before the corner, skip next three sts; repeat from * * around, join using slip stitch (ss) in first single crochet (sc) . Fasten off. In the end, weave.

Last Look:

EMBROIDERING CHAIN Stitches on Fabric
• Insert the needle at the beginning point from the back to the front, and pull through the fabric completely, leaving only a short tail.
• Pull your thread through by moving the needle from front to back one or two threads from your beginning place, leaving a tiny loop on the front end. Bring the thread to the front end and through the preferred-sized circle for the chain stitch.
• Grab the loop by pulling the thread back one or two threads from the previous place; drag the thread through to the back, leaving a loop for your next stitch.

Chapter 7

CROCHET FOR KIDS

CROCHET PUMPKIN PATTERN

SPECIAL STITCHES

If you would like to crochet a pumpkin stem for your pumpkin, you'll need to know the front post double crochet stitch. It's very similar to the double crochet stitch — you'll just insert your hook in a different spot.

Front Post Double Crochet: Yarn over, insert hook from front to back to front around the post of corresponding stitch below, yarn over and pull up a loop (3 loops on the hook). Yarn over, draw through 2 loops on hook (2 loops on the hook). Yarn over, draw through 2 loops on hook, again.

Row 1: Ch 31. Starting in the 2nd ch from the hook, and working in blo for all stitches, make 3 sl st, 6 sc, 12 hdc, 6 sc, 3 sl st. Turn. (30)

Row 2: Ch 1. Working in blo, 3 sl st, 6 sc, 12 hdc, 6 sc, 3 sl st. Turn. (30)

Repeat Row 2 until the piece measures 12 in long. (Measured across the center at the widest point.) I crocheted 40 rows.

Last Row: You can make the last row and seam the short sides in the same step. To do this, fold the short sides together, right sides facing out. Insert the hook through both the starting chain stitches and the back loops of the working stitches as you crochet the last row – all slip stitches.

Finishing

If you didn't join the sides as you worked the last row of crochet (as described in the previous section, join the sides with a mattress stitch. Then, turn the pumpkin so that the raised "V" shapes point down. With a matching piece of yarn and blunt yarn needle (I used the long yarn tail) sew a running stitch along the top edge.

Pull the ends of the yarn to gather the top edge. Tie a knot, cut the excess yarn, and weave in the ends.

Next, stuff the pumpkin with fiberfill through the bottom opening.

In the same way as before, sew a running stitch along the bottom edge. Pull the ends of the yarn to gather the bottom edge. Tie a knot, cut the excess yarn, and weave in the ends.

You can stop here, or you can make some additional stitches to create a sculpted, "squashed" pumpkin shape.

To do this, make some long stitches that run vertically between the stem end and the base of the pumpkin. I made four stitches down through the center of the pumpkin, overlapping them in an X shape (almost like sewing on a button.)

Pull these stitches with slight tension to give the pumpkin a more realistic shape. Knot the yarn to secure, and weave in the ends.

When it comes to attaching a stem to your pumpkin For a simple stem, you can use hot glue to attach a short twig or a cinnamon stick to the top of the pumpkin.

EASY CROCHET ELEPHANT

Legs – Make 2 in light gray

Chart for first 3 rounds:

- Rnd 1: 8 sc into magic ring. (8)
- Rnd 2: Inc in each st around. (16)
- Rnd 3: (Inc, sc 1) x8. (24)
- Rnd 4: Blsc in each st around. (24)
- Rnd 5: Sc in each st around. (24)
- Rnd 6: (Sc 6, inv dec) x3. (21)
- Rnd 7: (Sc 5, inv dec) x3. (18)
- Rnd 8: (Sc 4, inv dec) x3. (15)
- Rnds 9-15: Sc in each st around. (15)
- First 3 rounds + finished legs:

 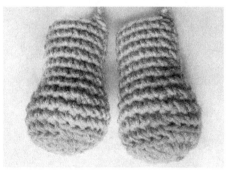

Arms – Make 2 in light gray:
Make a magic ring.
Rnd 1: 8 sc into the magic ring. (8)
Rnd 2: Inc in each st around. (16)
Rnd 3: (Inc in next st, sc 1) x8. (24)
Rnd 4: Blsc in each st around. (24)
Rnd 5: (Sc 4, inv dec) x3. Sc in last 6 sts. (21)

Rnd 6: (Sc 3, inv dec) x3. Sc in last 6 sts. (18)
Rnd 7: (Sc 2, inv dec) x3. Sc in last 6 sts. (15)

First 7 rnds of arms:
Rnds 8-12: Sc in each st around. (15)
Rnd 13: (Sc 3, inv dec) x3. (12)
Rnd 14: Sc in each st around. (12)

Rnd 15: (Sc 2, inv dec) x3. (9)
Rnds 16-17: Sc in each st around. (9)
Fasten off. Fill with stuffing until row 12. Sew the opening closed (see picture). Give the feet 3 "toes" by drawing a strand of yarn from below the blsc up to rnd 6. Do this twice, spaced apart by about 6 sts.

Body – in light gray
Make a magic ring.

- Rnd 1: 8 sc into magic ring. (8)
- Rnd 2: Inc in each st around. (16)
- Rnd 3: (Inc in next st, sc 1) x8. (24)
- Rnd 4: (Inc in next st, sc 2) x8. (32)
- Rnd 5: (Inc in next st, sc 3) x8. (40)
- Rnd 6: (Inc in next st, sc 4) x8. (48)
- Rnds 7-11: Sc in each st around. (48)
- Rnd 12: (Inv dec, sc 4) x8. (40)
- Rnds 13-14: Sc in each st around. (40)
- Rnd 15: (Inv dec, sc 3) x8. (32)
- Rnds 16-17: Sc in each st around. (32)
- Rnd 18: (Inv dec, sc 2) x8. (24)
- Rnd 19 and 20: Sc in each st around. (24)
- Fasten off. Fill with stuffing. Do not close the opening.

Tail – in light gray and dark gray
With light gray, ch 3.

- Rnd 1: 2 sc into the second ch from hook. 3 sc into next ch. Turn to work on the other side of the ch. 1 sc into other side of ch. (6)
- Rnds 2-10: Sc in each st around. (6)

Fasten off. Sew the opening closed (do not fill with stuffing). Cut some pieces of yarn from the dark gray and attach them into the first rnd of the tail like fringe.

Trunk – in light gray
Make a magic ring.

Rnd 1: 8 sc into magic ring. (8)
Rnd 2: Sc in each st around. (8)
Rnd 3: Sl st in next 4 sts, sc 4. (8)
Rnd 4: Sc in each st around. (8)
Rnd 5: Rep round 3. (8)
Rnd 6: Sl st in next 4 sts. Inc in each of the next 4 sts. (12)
Rnd 7: Sl st in next 4 sts, sc 8. (12)
Rnd 8: Sl st in next 4 sts, hdc 8. (12)
Rnd 9: Sl st in next 4 sts. (Hdc 3, hdc inc) x2. (14)
Rnd 10: Sc 4, hdc 10. (14)
Rnd 11: Sl st in next 4 sts. (Hdc 4, hdc inc) x2. (16)
Rnd 12: Sc 4, hdc 12. (16)
Rnd 13: Sl st in next 4 sts. (Hdc 3, hdc inc) x3. (19)
Rnd 14: Sc 4, hdc 15. (19)
Rnd 15: Sl st in next 4 sts, hdc 15. (19)
Rnd 16: Hdc in each st around. (19)

81

Ears – Make 2 in dark gray &
2 in light gray
Starting with dark gray yarn,
make a magic ring.

Row 1: Ch 2, 8 hdc into magic
ring. Ch 2 and turn. (8)
Row 2: Make 2 hdc in each st.
Ch 2 and turn. (16)
Row 3: (Hdc 1, 2 hdc in next
st) x8. Ch 2 and turn. (24)
Row 4: (Hdc 2, 2 hdc in next
st) x8. (32)

Fasten off.
For light gray ears, follow rnds 1 to 4 above. Do not fasten off.
Place the dark gray ear on top of the light gray ear and work
into both pieces together. Work the following rnd below to join
them together.
Joining Row: Ch 1, sc in next 7 sts (working through the layers
of both ears). 4 sc in next st. Sc in next 16 sts, 4 sc in next st. Sc
in last 7 sts. Fasten off.

Head – in light gray
Make a magic ring.

- Rnd 1: 8 sc into magic ring. (8)
- Rnd 2: Inc in each st around. (16)
- Rnd 3: (Inc in next st, sc 1) x8. (24)
- Rnd 4: (Inc in next st, sc 2) x8. (32)
- Rnd 5: (Inc in next st, sc 3) x8. (40)
- Rnd 6: (Inc in next st, sc 4) x8. (48)
- Rnds 7-12: Sc in each st around. (48)
- Attach eyes between round 4 and 5, with 10 sts in between them
- Rnd 13: (Sc 6, inv dec) x6. (42)
- Rnd 14: (Sc 5, inv dec) x6. (36)
- Rnd 15: (Sc 4, inv dec) x6. (30)
- Rnd 16: (Sc 3, inv dec) x6. (24)
- Rnd 17: (Sc 2, inv dec) x6. (18)
- Begin stuffing here.
- Rnd 18: (Sc 1, inv dec) x6. (12)
- Rnd 19: (Inv dec over next 2 sts) x6. (6)

Fasten off. Fill with stuffing. Sew the opening closed.
Finishing:

- Attach trunk and ears to the head.
- Join head and body together.
- Attach arms, legs, and tail.

CROCHET WHALE PATTERN

Body – in light blue
Make a magic ring.

- Rnd 1: Make 8 sc into ring. (8)
- Rnd 2: (Inc) 8x. (16)
- Rnd 3: (Sc 1, inc) x8. (24)
- Rnd 4: (Sc 2, inc) x8. (32)
- Rnd 5: Sc in each st around. (32)
- Rnd 6: Sc 12. (Sc 3, inc) x5. (37)

- Rnd 7: Sc 12. (Sc 4, inc) x5. (42)
- Rnd 8: (Sc 5, inc) x2. Sc 30. (44)
- Rnd 9: Sc in each st around. (44)
- Rnd 10: Sc 14. (Sc 5, inc) x5. (49)
- Rnd 11: Sc 14. (Sc 6, inc) x5. (54)
- Rnds 12-19: Sc in each st around. (54)

Attach eyes between rnds 14 and 15.

- Rnd 20: Sc 14. (Sc 6, inv dec) x5. (49)
- Rnd 21: Sc 14. (Sc 5, inv dec) x5. (44)
- Rnd 22: Sc in each st around. (44)
- Rnd 23: Sc 14. (Sc 4, inv dec) x5. (39)
- Rnd 24: Sc in each st around. (39)
- Rnd 25: (Sc 11, inv dec) x3. (36)
- Rnd 26: (Sc 4, inv dec) x3. (Sc 1, inv dec) x6. (27)
- Rnd 27: Sc in each st around. (27)
- Rnd 28: (Sc 7, inv dec) x3. (24)
- Rnd 29: Sl st 2, sc 16, sl st 6. (24)
- Rnds 30-31: Sc in each st around. (24)

Fill with stuffing.

- Rnd 32: Inv dec, sc, inv dec. Sc 14, inv dec, sc, inv dec. (20)
- Rnds 33-34: Sc in each st around. (20)
- Rnd 35: Inv dec, sc 1. Sc 14, sc 1. Inv dec. (18)
- Rnd 36: (Sc 4, inv dec) x3. (15)
- Rnd 37: Sc 4, inv dec, sc 2, inv dec, sc 5. (13)
- Rnds 38-39: Sc in each st around. (13)
- Rnd 40: Sc 6, inv dec, sc 5. (12)

Fill the rest with stuffing. Do not fasten off. Continue to work on the fluke.

Body: 1st fluke

Rnds 41-42: Sc 12. (12)
Rnd 43: (Inc) 6x. Skip next 6 sts. (12)
Rnd 44: Working in the first sc of last rnd, (sc 1, inc) x6. (18)

Skipping 6 sts to divide flipper in half:

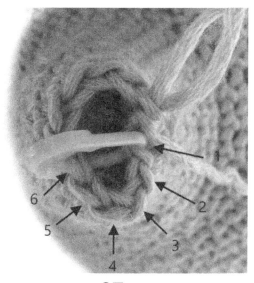

- Rnds 45-47: Sc in each st around. (18)
- Rnd 48: (Sc 1, inv dec) x6. (12)
- Rnds 49-50: Sc in each st around. (12)
- Rnd 51: (Inv dec) x6. (6)

Fasten off. Sew the opening closed. Do not fill with stuffing.

2nd fluke:
Attach the yarn into the 1st st from the 6 sts we skipped.

- Rnd 1: (Inc) 6x. (12)
- Rnds 2-9: Repeat rnds 44-51.

Fasten off and sew the opening closed.

First fluke + finished flukes:

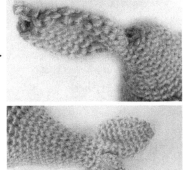

Flippers – in light blue
Make a magic ring.

- Rnd 1: 6 sc into ring. (6)
- Rnd 2: Sc 5, inc. (7)
- Rnd 3: Sc 5, 2 inc. (9)
- Rnd 4: Sc 5, (Sc 1, inc) x2. (11)
- Rnd 5: Sc 5, (Sc 2, inc) x2. (13)
- Rnd 6: Sc in each st around. (13)
- Rnd 7: Sl st in each st around.(13)

Fasten off. Do not fill with stuffing.
Finished flippers:

Blowhole – in yellow
First Side:
Make a magic ring.
- Rnd 1: 6 sc into ring. (6)
- Rnds 2-5: Sc in each st around. (6) Fasten off.

Second Side:
Make a magic ring.
- Repeat Rnds 1-5. Do not fasten off.
- Joining rnd 1: Insert the hook into a st from the last rnd of the first side and make a sc. Continue to make 5 more sc around this side (the side already fastened off). Make 6 sc around the other side. (12)

NOTE: be careful when joining that you don't accidentally work in the first st made 2x. If you end up with 13 sc, you have accidentally increased—take it out & try again.

- Joining Rnd 2: (Inv dec) x6. (6)
- Joining Rnds 3-4: Sc in each st around. (6)
- Fasten off. Fill with stuffing if desired (optional)

Joining 1st side and 2nd side with a sc + finished blowhole:

Finished belly:

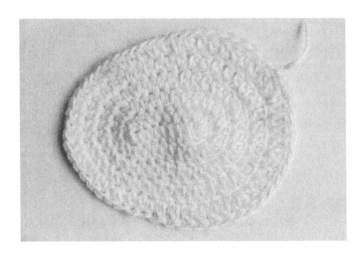

Finishing:
Attach the belly on the bottom of the Whale.
Attach Flippers between rnd 17 and 23 on each side.
Attach Blowhole between rnd 16 and 18.
Embroider the mouth with a black yarn in a nice way as you wish.
Embroider the eye with white yarn.

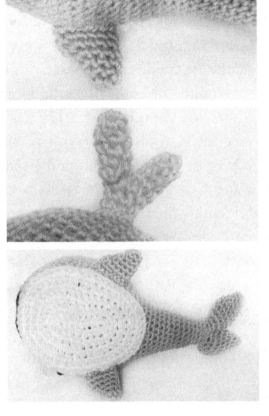

THE CROCHET GIRAFFE

Legs – Make 4 in brown & yellow
Make a magic ring.

- Rnd 1: With B, 6 sc into magic ring. (6)
- Rnd 2: Inc in each st around. (12)

Chart for the first 2 rnds of the leg

- Rnd 3: Blsc in each st around. (12)
- Rnds 4-5: Sc in each st around. (12)

Change to color Y.
Rnd 6: Sl st in each st around. (12)
After first 6 rnds:

- Rnds 7-11: Sc in each st around. (12)
- Rnd 12: Sl st in each st around. (12)

Fasten off and fill with stuffing. Do not sew the opening closed.

Finished legs:

Joining Legs
Chart to follow:

- Step 1: Attach the Y yarn with a sl st to the last rnd of the leg.
- Step 2: Ch 6. Insert the hook into a st from the 2nd leg. (see below)

Step 3: Make 12 sc around the 2nd leg. Sc 6 across the chs.
Step 4: Make 12 sc around the 1st leg. Sc 6 across the other side of the chs. Fasten off.

After sc row around legs and both sides of the chs

Follow the same steps to join the other two legs together.

Joining Both Sets of Legs
Chart to follow:

Attach the Y yarn with a sl st in the 4th st of the 12 sts around the leg (see the chart/photo.)

- Row 1: Ch 1. Sc 14, ch 1 and TURN. (14)
- Row 2. Sc 14, ch 1 and TURN. (14)
- Row 3: Hold both parts together and make 14 sc through both layers. (14)

Do not fasten off, but continue to make the body.

Joining two parts together with sc:

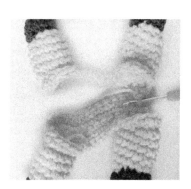

After join, there will be 50 sc sts for the first body rnd.

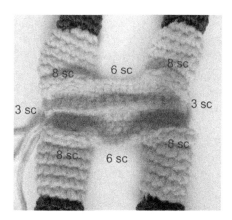

Body – in yellow
- Rnds 1-2: Sc in each st around the body. (50)
- Rnd 3: (Sc 1, inv dec) x2. Sc 35. (Sc 1, inv dec) x3. (45)
- Rnd 4: (Sc 1, inv dec) x3. Sc 25. (Inv dec, sc 1) x3. Sc in last 2 sts. (39)
- Rnd 5: Sc in each st around. (39)

Fill the legs with stuffing.
- Rnd 6: (Inv dec) x3. Sc 25, (inv dec) x3. Sc in last 2 sts. (33)

Body so far:

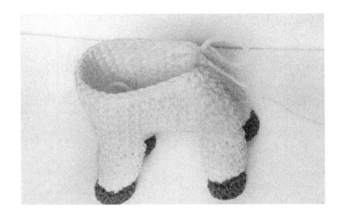

- Rnd 7: (Inv dec) x4. Sc 15, (inv dec) x5. (24)
- Rnd 8: (Sc 4, inv dec) x4. (20)
- Rnd 9: (Sc 3, inv dec) x4. (16)
- Rnds 10-15: Sc in each st around. (16)
- Begin filling the body with stuffing here.
- Rnd 16: (Sc 6, inv dec) x2. (14)
- Rnds 17-20: Sc in each st around. (14)
- Rnd 21: (Sc 5, inv dec) x2. (12)
- Rnds 22-23: Sc in each st around. (12)

Fasten off. Fill the rest of the body with stuffing.

Finished Body

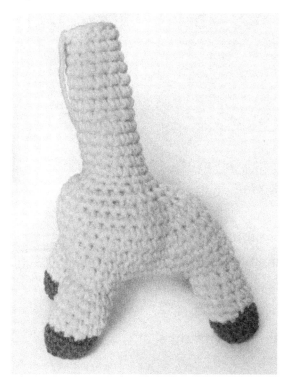

Horns – Make 2 using brown & yellow
With B, make a magic ring.

- Rnd 1: Sc 6 into ring. (6)
- Rnd 2: Inc in each st around. (12)
- Rnds 3-4: Sc in each st around. (12)
- Rnd 5: (Inv dec) x6. (6)

Change to Y color.
- Rnds 6-8: Sc in each st around.(6)
Fasten off and fill with stuffing.

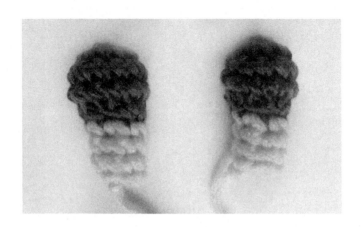

Ears – Make 2 in yellow
Make a magic ring.

- Rnd 1: 8 sc into ring. (8)
- Rnd 2: Inc in each st around. (16)
- Rnd 3: (Sc 1, inc) x8. (24)
- Rnd 4: (Sc 2, inc) x8. (32)

Ch 1 and fasten off without sl st.

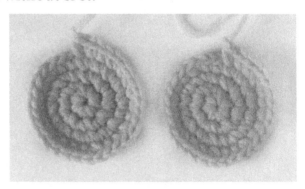

Head – in yellow
Make a magic ring.

- Rnd 1: 6 sc into ring. (6)
- Rnd 2: Inc in each st around. (12)
- Rnd 3: (Sc 1, inc) x6. (18)
- Rnd 4: (Sc 2, inc) x6. (24)

- Rnd 5: (Sc 3, inc) x6. (30)
- Rnds 6-15: Sc in each st around. (30)

Attach eyes between rnd 12 and 13, with 11 sts in between.

- Rnd 16: (Sc 3, inv dec) x6. (24)
- Rnd 17: (Sc 2, inv dec) x6. (18)
- Rnd 18: (Sc 1, inv dec) x6. (12)

Fill with stuffing.
- Rnd 19: (Inv dec) x6. (6)
Fasten off and sew the opening closed.

Spots – in brown
Make a magic ring.
Small – make 2
- Rnd 1: 6 sc into ring. (6)

Medium – make 4
Rnd 1: Rep small rnd 1.
Rnd 2: Inc in each st around. (12)

Large – make 2
Rnds 1-2: Rep medium rnds 1-2.
Rnd 3: (Sc 1, inc) x6. (18)

Tail – in both colors
Make a magic ring.
Rnd 1: With Y, 6 sc into ring. (6)
Rnds 2-6: Sc in each st around. (6)
Attach some pieces of B yarn on the end of the tail like fringe.

Finished tail:

Finishing:
Attach ears next to eyes, between rnd 14 and 15. Attach horns between rnd 15 and 17, next to ears. Embroider mouth between rnd 7 and 8.
Attach spots and tail on the body according to pictures (or to your liking).
Sew head and body together.

Chapter 8

IMPORTANT THINGS FOR BEGINNERS

2-dc cluster:

 Yarn over, place the hook in specified stitch and pull up one loop, yarn over (YO) and pull thru two loops on the hook, yarn over, embed
hook with in the same stitch to pull up another loop, yarn over (YO) and pull thru two loops, yarn over (YO) and pull all three loops on the hook.

3-dc cluster: Yarn over, place hook in the specified stitch to pull up one loop, yarn over (YO) and pull thru two loops onto the hook, (yarn over, place the hook with in the same stitch and pull up another loop, yarn over (YO) and pull thru two more loops) twice, yarn over (YO) and pull thru all four loops on the hook.

Adjustable ring: leave a 6 inch (15 cm) tail, create a loop using the yarn and keep it in your left hand with the working yarn (WY) over the index finger

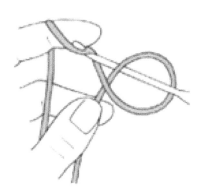

DRAWING YOUR WORKING yarn through the loop, you just created so that you only have one loop on your hook.

WORK THE REQUIRED NUMBER of build-up chains for the 1st stitch , then work stitches in the circle as directed (i.e. single, double, or triple crochet). Work every stitch over the loop yarn and the tail yarn .

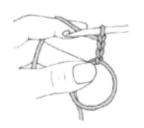  

WHEN THE FINAL STITCH has been crocheted, remove the extra tail from the loop and draw it up to finish the loop. You could leave an empty hole in the middle, or firmly pull it up to close the ring.

Back loop vs. front loop: When you look at your work, the back loop is the one farther away. The front loop is the one that is closer to you

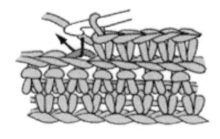 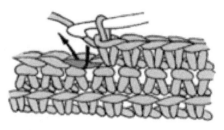

BLDC (DOUBLE CROCHET back loop): Create one double crochet into the rear loop only.

BLhdc (back loop half double crochet): Create one half double crochet into the rear loop only.

BLhdc2tog (back loop half double crochet two stitches together): Yarn over, embed hook into the rear loop of your succeeding stitch and pull up one loop, yarn over, add hook into the back loop of your next stitch and pull up one loop, yarn over again and pull through all five loops on the hook.

BLsc (back loop single crochet): Create one single crochet into the rear loop only.

BLsc2tog (back loop single crochet two stitches together): (Embed hook into the rear loop of next stitch and pull up one loop) twice, yarn over (YO) and pull through all three loops on the hook.

BL slip st (back loop slip st): Create one slip stitch into the rear loop only.

Back post vs. front post: To create a back post stitch, enter the hook from the back to the front to the back around the post of stitch showed.

To work a front post stitch, create the hook from the front to the back to the front around post of stitch showed.

dc (double crochet): Yarn over, embed hook into the stitch or space showed, and pull up one loop — three loops on the hook (yarn over, pull yarn through two of the loops on the hook) twice.

dc2tog (double crochet 2 together): (Yarn over, add the hook into next stitch or space and pull up one loop, yarn over, pull through two loops) twice, yarn over (YO) and pull through all three loops on the hook.

fdc (foundation double crochet): Start with a slip knot on your hook, chain 3, yarn over, insert hook in 3rd chain from your hook, yarn over (YO) and pull up one loop, yarn over (YO) and draw through one of the loop — chain made, (yarn over again and draw through two loops) twice — double crochet created. For each subsequent fdc, yarn over, insert hook under two loops of chain at the bottom of stitch last created, yarn over (YO) and pull up loop, yarn over again and draw through one of the loop — chain made, (yarn over again and draw through two loops) twice — double crochet made.

Front Loop Double Crochet (FLDC): Create one double crochet into your front loop only.

Front Loop Half Double Crochet (FLHDC): Create one half double crochet into your front loop only.

Front Loop Single Crochet (FLSC): Make one single crochet into your front loop only.

Foundation Single Crochet (FSC): Start by creating a slip knot on your hook, chain 2, embed hook into 2nd chain from hook, *yarn over (YO) and pull up one loop, yarn over (YO) and pull through one of the loop — one chain made, yarn over (YO) and pull through two loops — 1 fsc made**. For each subsequent fsc, insert your hook into the chain at the base of the previous fsc, repeat from * to ** for the desired length

PICOT-2: Chain 2, slip stitch in 2nd chain from hook.

Picot-3: Chain 3, slip stitch in 3rd chain from hook.

Picot-4: Chain 4, slip stitch in 4th chain from hook.

sc2tog (single crochet two stitches together): (Insert hook into next stitch and pull up one loop) twice, yarn over (YO) and pull through all three loops on the hook.

TSS (Tunisian simple stitch):

• Chain the required number.

• Row 1: Enter hook in 2nd chain from the hook, yarn over (YO) and pull up one loop, (embed hook into the next chain, yarn over, and pull up another loop) across — forward row finished; yarn over, pull through 1 loop on hook, (yarn over, pull through two loops on the hook) until one loop rests — return row ended

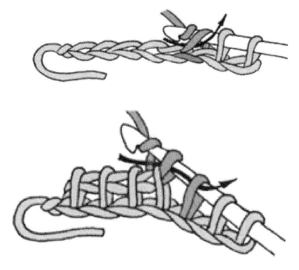

• Row 2: Jump the first vertical bar, enter hook under next vertical bar, yarn over, pull up one loop (embed hook under next vertical bar, yarn over, pull up another loop) across; work loops off using return row—repeat Row two for the pattern.

• TSS bind off (worked on the forward row): Enter hook under the second vertical bar from hook, yarn over, and pull through both the loops. You now have one loop on your hook. *Embed hook under next vertical bar, yarn over, pull through both the loops; repeat from * until all stitches are bound of sf.

Chapter 9

TIPS FOR EVERY NOVICE CROCHETER

Crocheting doesn't have to be difficult to sit back and do, but it can be difficult to pronounce and, in some cases, even more difficult to write. All of these crocheting tips, tricks, and hacks can greatly enhance your life!

Mellow Itchy Yarn: Stiffness is a characteristic of low-cost yarns. A stiff, scratchy scarf would be exceedingly uncomfortable to wear. To soften the yarn for this, use shampoo or any other favorite conditioner. The scarf would also smell exactly like the shampoo you used, which is a bonus.

Alternate between hooks to achieve the Best Stitch results: Change your hooks if you discover that the stitches are either too loose or too close together. If the stitches become too loose, try a smaller crochet hook. If the crochet hooks are too little, use a larger one. Even though it looks simple, many students could forget to alter the hook!

Though it's best to avoid doing so in the middle of your endeavor. If the threads are not the right size, different guidelines must be followed, but you still want the stitches to be as seamless as possible in your design.

Complete a Project: To create a product with a neat finish, weave the ends of your yarn into your crochet motifs as you work on them.

A gauge for crochet: Do not fall for the deception that crochet gauges are not worth your time, money, or effort. That is a total fabrication.

Never Leave Anything Behind: Create a loop of your last stitch that is extra lengthy in case you are ever unexpectedly stopped. When you return to your project, you'll know exactly where you left off because of this! Perfect!

Check Hand Cramping: Joint discomfort and weariness in the hands and arms are definitely issues for new crocheters. However, preventing it is much simpler than you might think. Every 30 minutes, take a break and relax your hands and wrists to prevent tiredness. Make sure your arms, back, and spine are at ease while working on your job. Nobody enjoys having sore necks.

Continuing With More Difficult Projects: Are you tired of only being able to produce long chains or snakes in your attempts to learn how to crochet? There are several straightforward crochet patterns available for beginners that will direct you toward the following stage of your crocheting journey. Make your own accessories like a cap, headband, and jewelry. There are countless opportunities.

never-iron crocheted items No matter how alluring it may be, it is never a good idea to iron the stitches on your design. The thread will "fry" in the iron, destroying your stitches and all of your hard work!

Reduce Supply Costs: Keep an index card in your pocket with your assortment of hooks, yarns, and other crocheting supplies that you've stashed away at home. This guarantees that if you're shopping in a craft store, you won't accidently take anything you've already purchased.

Knitting Storage: Do you need somewhere to put your crochet hooks in? Carriers for portable toothbrushes or pencil bags are excellent options.

MISTAKES CROCHETS MAKE AND SOLUTION

If you're only starting to learn or you have decades of experience, everyone is capable of repeating the same error. There's no embarrassment going down on these rising crochet errors! Now, it's good to be mindful of these time killers because we must be cautious about eliminating the stuff that will make our plans a mess.

Crocheting In Your Front Loop Only: It is very simple to make that error if you are inexperienced in crocheting. It's handy to know where to put the hook in every stitch; it's the foundation of this art. This error may occur as you have not entirely learned how you were trained to crochet, or for the reason that your hook slips occasionally. You are not experienced enough to realize the mistake immediately.

An easy way to remedy this error is to invest some additional time evaluating which row you are dealing with. It may sound boring, but currently that you understand the universal law of crocheting underneath both the loops (unless clearly instructed not to), then you can always ensure the stitches are well working before it is second nature.

Your Design Keeps Getting Broader And Broader: That is the one error that everybody makes at minimum once. I hope you can recall when you began the design and thinking, "It's going to be very quick, it's only going to keep repeating the very same stitch again and again!

"And after an hour and a half, you notice your cover is now an octagon rather than a rectangle! This problem happens because the stitches are not counted, and you ended up doing more stitches than you require. You could have doubled into one stitch, or you could accidentally work an additional stitch in the turning chain. Counting your stitches is the best way to avoid this disaster!

You can count every row as you complete it, or you may keep a close watch on the form of your project. Do not lose precious time working fast, and then remember that you inserted an additional stitch for ten rows back.

Miscounting Or Not Counting Your Row: This stage, and the previous, is all about not losing your precious time. Much like when you work, you have to calculate your stitches, so you do need to check the number.

If you make several times the same error, you've primarily just made it and then frogged an entire 2nd scarf. Using a row tracker is the most straightforward response to your problem. That may be a sophisticated automated row tracker that records every row with a single click, or you can go to the old fashioned way and use a pencil and paper to put a little check for each row you finish.

Combining U.S. and U.K. crochet terminology: What is referred to as a single crochet (sc) in the U.S. is referred to as a double crochet (dc) in the U.K. It's crucial to do your study on the template with that in mind before you start. If the pattern does not make it clear, ask the designer for confirmation. On the other hand, if you're a designer, it's always VERY important to be explicit with the terminology you employ.

When pursuing a crochet design, yarn weight is important to consider. If you use a different size yarn and expect the results to be similar to the pattern, this is a mistake. You should expect the gauge and finished piece to look very different if you wish to make a thick scarf using a pattern that calls for a # 6 yarn but you only have a # 5.

Every design is created with a certain yarn in mind, thus the only weight variation that will affect the outcome is that. Use your gauge palette if you like the yarn you have on hand and want to use it. It will determine what design modifications you might need to do in order to get it as similar as possible.

Using the Wrong Size Hook: This error is closely related to the previous one. The project outcome will be significantly changed if the hook is used in the incorrect size. Each pattern is created with a specific size of hook in mind, so changing any of that will result in stitching that is either too tight or too loose.

To make sure you have the correct scale, carefully study the pattern: Don't forget to swatch your gauge as well! You may not be aware that the hook you have in your hand is the incorrect one, and you have saved yourself a ton of time by avoiding having to restart an entire project.

Not Reading the Instructions in Full: Before starting a brilliant new design, spending time reading through each paragraph is the very last thing you want to do. Start by gathering your yarn and pin. With some experience working with crochet patterns, it's obvious that failing to understand the design first is a grave error. Maybe it doesn't change much every time, but if you didn't read the description beforehand, you might be perplexed by a trickier move.

You can practice a brand-new stitch advance throughout your first reading of the template. Although you don't have to memorize every move, reading through a pattern is similar to studying for an exam before you record it. An excellent method to start a new crochet project is with confidence.

Not knowing where to place the first stitch or incorrectly counting the chain:

The cornerstone of a crochet item is that first chain, which is also maybe the least enjoyable part of each design. One of the hardest things to learn while crocheting is chain learning, which is also one of the first things you'll do.

Chaining mistakes frequently involve not knowing where to place the starting stitch. If you don't count each stitch (see mistake #2), you'll end up with too many or too few stitches, and the project will fail. Learn how to chain and count chains in order to avoid becoming stuck in this situation or find a solution.

Making No Gauge Swatches: It's important to start using the swatch gauge right away. By adopting a design, this simple square will help you save time and energy and make it much easier for you to follow your patterns. The gauge specifies the stress required to create the proper design.

Remember to create some gage swatches (and utilize them in your models) and, if you feel that the stress is unusual, take the opportunity to raise or lower your hook size. For instance:

Leaving No Long Yarn Tail at the End: In the end, weaving may be the aspect of crocheting that everyone dislikes the least. No, you cannot simply cut the yarn in a sad manner and hope that no one notices, only to fail because the string is too short.

There is no difference between cutting a thread, adding a new yarn ring, or switching out different colors of yarn; you just need to make sure you have enough to knit with.

Printed in Great Britain
by Amazon

39079210R00066